The Eclectic Witch's
Grimoire
A Customizable Compendium of Magic

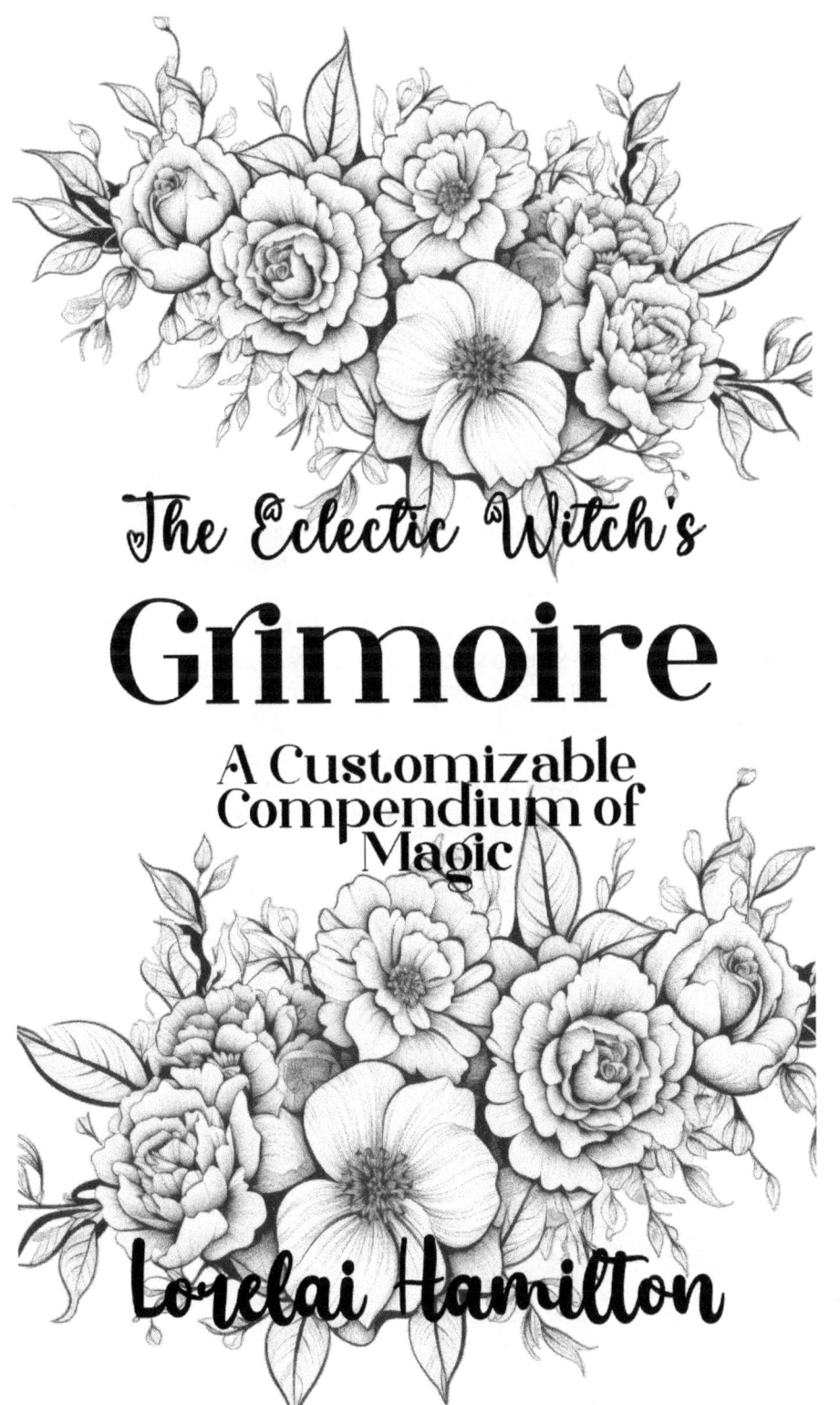

The Eclectic Witch's Grimoire

A Customizable Compendium of Magic

Lorelai Hamilton

The Eclectic Witch's Grimoire© 2024 by Lorelai Hamilton
Rainbow Quartz Publishing

ALL RIGHTS RESERVED. NO PART OF THIS BOOK MAY BE REPRODUCED, STORED IN A RETRIEVAL SYSTEM, OR TRANSMITTED BY ANY MEANS WHATSOEVER WITHOUT THE WRITTEN PERMISSION OF THE AUTHOR EXCEPT FOR THE USE OF BRIEF QUOTATIONS IN A BOOK REVIEW. THIS IS A WORK OF FICTION. ALL THE CHARACTERS, NAMES, PLACES, INCIDENTS, ORGANIZATIONS, AND DIALOGUE IN THIS NOVEL ARE EITHER THE PRODUCTS OF THE AUTHORS IMAGINATION OR ARE USED FICTIONALLY. ANY RESEMBLANCE TO ACTUAL PERSONS, EVENTS, OR LOCALES IS ENTIRELY COINCIDENTAL.

COVER ART BY RAINBOW QUARTZ PUBLISHING
IG: RAINBOW QUARTZ PUBLISHING

HTTPS://RQPUBLISHING.COM/

ISBN: 978-1-961714-27-4

Additional Books by Rainbow Quartz Publishing

Lorelai Hamilton

- Tarot Tales and Magic Spells: Demystifying Tarot Readings and Meanings One Story at a Time
- Teenage Tarot
- The Teenage Witch's Grimoire: Spells, Rituals, and Mystical Knowledge
- Tarot Reflection Journal: Coloring The Tarot
- Teenage Tarot : Unlock Your Inner Magic
- The Art of Manifestation Journal: From Belief to Reality, Rewrite Your Story Today
- Dream Journal: For Capturing Dreams From The In Between

Miranda Levi

- From A Youth A Fountain Did (Fountain of Youth 1)
- The Sea Withdrew (Fountain of Youth 2)
- A Tear In Time
- Mo(ther) Na(ture)
- In Orion's Hands: a collection of poetry

Jackson Anhalt

- From The 911 Files: True confessions from behind the phone

Isla Watts

- A Fairy Bad Day (Mythiverse 1)
- Surprise! You're A Vampire (Mythiverse 2)
- Gorgeous, Gorgeous, Gorgons (Mythiverse 3)
- Mork The Handsome Orc (Mythiverse 4)
- Adopted By Werewolves (Mythiverse 5)

Jax Wilder

- Sleighed by Love (Coral Cove 1)
- Harvesting Love (Coral Cove 2)
- Dawning Desire (Coral Cove 3)
- The Perfect Lover Spell (Coral Cove 4)

This book is for Jackson. Your unwavering belief in my potential has been the catalyst for countless adventures and triumphs.

Magic resides within us all, waiting to be summoned.

Thank you for being a guiding light, for your steadfast support, and for being the person who consistently breathes life into dreams. You embody the magic you inspire in others.

The Eclectic Witch's
Grimoire

Book Blessing

Book Blessing

A book blessing is a ritual or invocation performed to imbue a book, with positive energy, protection, and spiritual significance. This ritual is intended to consecrate the book and ensure that it serves as a sacred and potent tool for the practitioner's magical work.

The specific details of a book blessing can vary depending on the tradition, belief system, and personal preferences of the practitioner. However, common elements often include:

Cleansing: The book may be cleansed or purified using elements such as incense, holy water, or consecrated herbs to remove any negative energies or impurities.

Invocation of Divine Guidance: Prayers, invocations, or affirmations may be recited to invoke the divine or spiritual forces for protection, guidance, and empowerment.

Consecration: The practitioner may perform rituals to consecrate the book, dedicating it to a particular deity, spirit, or higher power and charging it with positive energy.

Symbolic Actions: Symbolic actions, gestures, or offerings may be performed to symbolize the book's sanctity and significance, such as lighting candles, anointing with oils, or placing sacred symbols or talismans within its pages.

Personalization: The practitioner may personalize the book blessing by infusing it with their intentions, goals, and aspirations for their magical practice, as well as any specific blessings or protections they wish to invoke.

The purpose of a book blessing in a grimoire is to establish a sacred connection between the practitioner and the book, empowering them to access its wisdom, knowledge, and magical potential with reverence and respect.

Table Of Contents

Content   Page #

Table Of Contents

Content	Page #

Table Of Contents

Content	Page #

Table Of Contents

Content   Page #

My Beliefs

Dedication

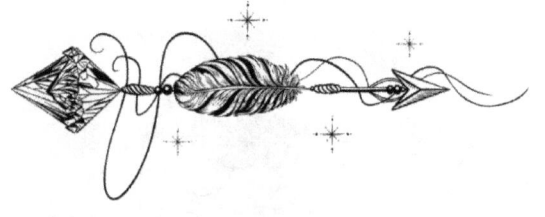

Dedication

Types of Witches

Augery: Specializes in interpreting omens, signs, and symbols.
Baby Witch: A beginner witch exploring different practices and traditions.
Celtic: Studies and worships Celtic deities and practices Celtic magic.
Ceremonial Witch: Emphasizes elaborate rituals and ceremonial magic.
Cosmic Witch: Draws on astrology and celestial energies in their magical practice.
Coven Based: Works as part of a group of witches, combining their powers to create stronger spells and rituals, often led by a high priestess.
Crystal Witch: Utilizes the power of crystals and stones in their magic, focusing on manifestation and energy work.
Dianic: An offshoot of Wicca that emphasizes female deities and women's spirituality.
Gray Witch: Balances between "white" and "black" magic, using both for various purposes.
Eclectic Witch: Incorporates various magical practices and beliefs into their own unique path.
Faery: Draws from folklore and works closely with fairies and nature spirits.
Folk Witch: Practices folk magic passed down through family or community traditions.
Green: Centers magic around herbalism, plant-based practices, and gardening.
Hearth: Focuses on home-based magic and domestic rituals.
House Witch: Similar to a hearth witch, but with a specific focus on making the home a magical space.
Hedge: Often a solitary practitioner who specializes in herbalism and plant magic.
Hellenic: Worships and works with the gods and goddesses of ancient Greece.
Hereditary: Practices handed down through family generations.
Kitchen Witch: Incorporates magic into cooking and baking, focusing on the kitchen as a sacred space.
Lunar: Works with lunar cycles and phases in their magical practices.
Modern: Embraces a diverse range of magical practices and traditions.
Norse: Draws from the traditions and mythology of Scandinavia and Norse gods.
Sea Witch: Specializes in water-based magic. Has a special connection to the ocean and practices water magic.
Secular: Practices magic without a focus on worshiping deities.
Sex Witch: Practices sex magic, incorporating arousal and orgasm into manifestation rituals.
Shaman: Enters altered states of consciousness to communicate with spirits and perform healing.
Solitary Witch: Practices alone, following their own path within witchcraft.
Wicca: A modern pagan witchcraft tradition with its own rituals, beliefs, and practices.

Alter & Elements

Witches Are

>>A witch serves as a conduit between the physical and spiritual realms, acting as a bridge connecting the two.

>>They symbolize the ideal world, striving to manifest harmony and balance in both their practice and the world around them.

>>In tune with the natural rhythms of the world, a witch possesses the ability to perceive and work with energy.

>>Drawing from both ancient wisdom and modern knowledge, they continuously refine and enhance their craft.

>>Whether working alone or within a coven, which is a group of witches with unique traditions and practices, a witch weaves magic to manifest their intentions.

>>Embracing diverse paths and traditions, there is no singular "right way" for a witch to practice their craft.

>>A witch commits themselves wholeheartedly to their craft and the betterment of the world, approaching their dedication with utmost seriousness.

Witch's Alter

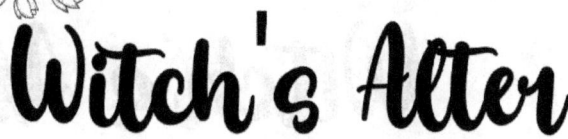

Your Witch's Altar serves as the focal point for your rituals and worship, aiding in concentration and mindfulness throughout your practice. It houses sacred tools, blessings, offerings, spell components, and ritual aids.

Selecting Your Altar Site:
Choose a location within your home that's easily accessible yet away from distractions like children and pets. Your Altar should serve as a reminder of your spiritual journey, whether it's a permanent fixture or assembled specifically for ritual purposes.

What Belongs on Your Altar?
There are no strict rules regarding Altar contents, but here are some traditional suggestions:

Creating Your Altar:
Crafting an Altar can be straightforward and practical, especially for beginners. Focus on setting up a space for standard rituals, Sabbats (celebrations of the Sun), and Esbats (celebrations of the Moon).

Common Alter Items:
>>**Altar Cloth:** Decorates the ritual space; choose a design or color that resonates with you.
>>**Deity Representations:** Use oracle cards, candles, statues, or other significant objects.
Elemental
>>**Representations:** Include items symbolizing Air, Earth, Fire, and Water.
>>**Traditional Tools**: Athame, cauldron, wand, pentacle, candles, chalice, etc.
>>**Miscellaneous Items:** Crystals, charms, divination tools, spell components, and decorations.

Witch's Alter

Your Witch's Altar serves as the focal point for your rituals and worship, aiding in concentration and mindfulness throughout your practice. It houses sacred tools, blessings, offerings, spell components, and ritual aids.

Arranging Your Altar:
Follow your intuition when arranging your Altar; there are no strict guidelines. Here are some layout suggestions:

Deity Representations: Place central deities towards the back, surrounded by other objects.
Elemental Representations: Align elements with corresponding quarters or cardinal directions.
Traditional Tools: Arrange tools for easy access and align them according to masculine or feminine symbolism.

Safety Considerations:
Prioritize safety when placing items on your Altar, especially those involving flames or liquids. Taller items like candles should be placed towards the back, while smaller items can be nearer to the front. Larger items like cauldrons can be centered, to the side, or on the floor adjacent to the Altar.

Elements

In the realm of magic, the Classical Elements—Earth, Air, Fire, Water, and Spirit—are revered as the fundamental building blocks of the Universe. These Elements permeate everything in existence and govern the perpetual cycle of nature's transformation.

Witches hold the Elements in deep reverence due to their profound natural influence. They integrate the Elements into their rituals and weave them into their daily lives, recognizing the omnipresent essence of Earth, Air, Water, Fire, and Spirit.

At the onset of a ritual, the Elements are invoked and utilized to cast the sacred circle. Each Element corresponds to one of the cardinal directions: Earth in the North, Air in the East, Water in the West, and Fire in the South. By facing each direction, practitioners call upon the spirit of the respective Element, a ritual known as "calling the quarters." Upon completion of the circle, the Elements are respectfully dismissed.

On the Altar, each Element is symbolized by specific ritual tools: the pentacle represents Earth, candles symbolize Fire, the chalice embodies Water, and wands signify Air. While practitioners may include multiple representations of each Element, it's recommended to maintain balance by aligning them with the quarters and ensuring at least one tool for each Element is present.

Herbs, crystals, and colors possess Elemental associations as well, allowing practitioners to intuitively select natural objects to represent the Elements and enhance their magical workings.

Incorporating other traditions such as Astrology or Tarot, which also carry strong Elemental connections, can deepen one's understanding and integration of the Elements into their practice. Each Zodiac sign corresponds to an Element, and the four suits in Tarot are linked to the Classical Elements.

Successful engagement with the Elements entails continual exploration and cultivation of a personal relationship with each Element, understanding their nuances, and discerning their significance in individual practice.

With myriad elemental correspondences available, practitioners are encouraged to embrace those that resonate most deeply with their spiritual journey.

Water

Direction - West

Rules - Emotion, intuition, psychic abilities, love, deep feelings, the unconscious mind, fertility, tides, lunar energy, self-healing, reflection

Time - Twilight

Season - Fall

Colors - Blue, aqua, silver, turquoise

Zodiac - Cancer, Scorpio, Pisces

Tools - Sea shells, ocean water, seaweed, hag stones, chalice, cup, cauldron

Virtues - Love, compassion, receptivity, flexibility, forgiveness

Vices - Indifference, depression, instability, moodiness

Crystals - Amethyst, aquamarine, beryl, blue fluorite, blue topaz, blue tourmaline, lapis lazuli, opal, pearl, sodalite
Metals - Mercury, silver

Plants - Aloe, apple, chamomile, ferns, gardenia, jasmine, lemon, lilac, lily, lotus, moss, passion flower, rose, seaweed, thyme, willow

Ruling planet - Moon, Neptune, Pluto

Water

▽

West

Earth

Direction - North

Rules - Grounding, strength, healing, nature, animals, success, stability, sturdiness, foundations, empathy, fertility, death, rebirth, wisdom

Time - Midnight
Season - Winter

Colors - Green, brown, black, white, gold

Zodiac - Taurus, Virgo, Capricorn

Tools - Pentacle, salt, crystals, dirt, herbs, wood, plants, flowers

Virtues - Centeredness, patience, truthfulness, dependability, thoroughness

Vices - Dullness, laziness, inconsiderateness

Crystals - Emerald, jet, tourmaline, quartz, granite, bedrock, salt, peridot, onyx, jasper, azurite, amethyst

Metals - Iron, lead
Plants - Cedar, cypress, honeysuckle, ivy, magnolia, grains, patchouli, primrose, sage, nuts, oak

Ruling planet - Venus, Saturn

Earth

Air

Direction - East

Rules - Mind, clarity, wisdom, knowledge, logic, abstract thought, wind,
 higher consciousness, divination, psychic work, intuition, memory

Time - Dawn
Season - Spring

Colors - Yellow, gold, white, light blue

Zodiac - Gemini, Libra, Aquarius

Tools - Feather, wand, staff, incense, censer, pen, broom, bell

Virtues - Intelligent, practical, optimistic

Vices - Impulsive, frivolous, easily fooled

Crystals - Topaz, amber, citrine, jasper, agate

Metals - Tin, copper

Plants - Acacia, anise, aspen, clover, frankincense, lavender, lemongrass, myrrh, pine, vervain, yarrow

Ruling planet - Mercury, Jupiter, Uranus

Air

Fire

Direction - South

Rules - Energy, will, healing, destruction, courage, strength, physical exercise, self-knowledge, power, passion, sexuality, divinity, heat, flame, light

Time - Noon

Season - Summer

Colors - Red, orange, gold, white

Zodiac - Aries, Leo, Sagittarius

Tools - Candle, lamp, athame, sword, dagger, burned herbs

Virtues - Courage, enthusiasm, willpower

Vices - Anger, jealousy, hatred

Crystals - Fire opal, ruby, garnet, red jasper, bloodstone, lava stone, quartz, tiger's eye, agate

Metals - Gold, brass

Plants - Allspice, basil, cinnamon, garlic, juniper, hibiscus, nettle, onion, red/orange peppers, red poppies, thistle

Ruling planet - Sun, Mars

Zodiac Signs

Aries March 21 - April 19

Taurus April 20 - May 20

Gemini May 21 - June 20

Cancer June 21 - July 22

Leo July 23 - August 22

Virgo August 23 - Sept 22

Libra September 23 - October 22

Scorpio October 23 - November 21

Sagittarius November 22 - December 21

Capricorn December 22 - January 19

Aquarius January 20 - February 18

Pisces February 19 - March 20

Zodiac

Zodiac signs are imbued with unique qualities categorized as Cardinal, Fixed, and Mutable.

Understanding your sign's quality can offer insights into when to plan your magic and the type of magic to focus on during specific Zodiac periods.

Each quality corresponds to a different stage of the seasons: **Cardinal represents the beginning, Fixed denotes the middle, and Mutable signifies the end.** Here's a breakdown of each quality:

Cardinal Signs: These individuals are born at the start of the season. They are independent, driven, and highly motivated, sometimes displaying impatience in their endeavors.

Fixed Signs: People born in the middle of the season fall under this category. They tend to be consistent, reliable, and steadfast, though they can also exhibit stubbornness at times.

Mutable Signs: Those born at the end of the season possess flexibility, resourcefulness, and creativity. While they adapt easily to change, they may sometimes lack perseverance.

Here's how the signs align with their qualities:
Cardinal: Aries, Cancer, Libra, Capricorn
Fixed: Taurus, Leo, Scorpio, Aquarius
Mutable: Gemini, Virgo, Sagittarius, Pisces

Zodiac

Additionally, the Zodiac signs are associated with the four classical elements: Fire, Earth, Air, and Water, each reflecting distinct personality traits:

Fire Signs: Passionate and energetic, with strong emotions and assertive natures. They are highly active and dynamic.

Earth Signs: Grounded, practical, and dependable, with a knack for being skillful and down-to-earth.

Air Signs: Creative and adventurous, with a penchant for intellectual pursuits and social interactions. They thrive on communication and relationships.

Water Signs: Emotional and sensitive, often possessing psychic abilities. They are deeply attuned to their feelings and intuition.

Here's how the signs align with the elements:

Fire: Aries, Leo, Sagittarius
Earth: Taurus, Virgo, Capricorn
Air: Gemini, Libra, Aquarius
Water: Cancer, Scorpio, Pisces

Understanding both the qualities and elemental influences of your Zodiac sign can provide valuable insights into your personality, strengths, and areas for growth.

Planets/Energy/Symobls

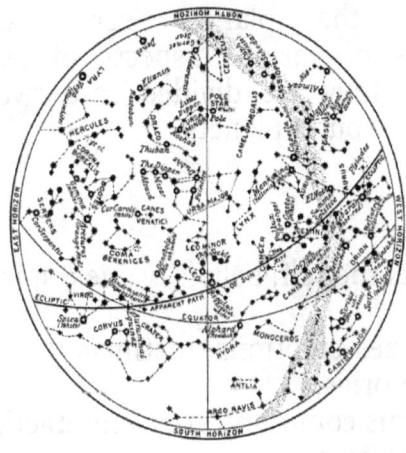

Understanding astrology goes beyond just knowing your Sun Sign; it involves delving into the complexities of the planets. There are ten planets in astrology, including the Sun and Moon, which are technically considered luminaries rather than planets. However, in astrological practice, they are treated as planets.

In your birth chart, each planet holds significance, offering insights into your deepest beliefs, values, desires, and emotional nature. When considering magical timing, it's essential to understand the role of the planets.

For magical rituals, you can focus on harnessing the energy of a specific planet based on its significance in your birth chart or its position on the ecliptic at a given time of the year. Utilize online resources to explore each planet's energy and symbolism thoroughly.

Before incorporating planetary energies into your rituals, take time to familiarize yourself with the unique characteristics and influences of each planet. This deeper understanding will enhance the effectiveness of your magical practice.

Planets/Energy/Symobls

In astrology, the planets serve as symbolic representations of various aspects of our lives and consciousness. They are divided into two categories: inner planets and outer planets.

Inner Planets:

Sun: Represents the self, beliefs, values, spirit, and inner strength.
Moon: Symbolizes emotions, instincts, the unconscious mind, and memories.
Mercury: Governs communication, interaction, intellect, and mental processes.
Venus: Rules over love, relationships, social connections, beauty, money, and harmony.
Mars: Influences action, confidence, ego, impulse, and physical energy.

Outer Planets:

Jupiter: Symbolizes wealth, growth, abundance, expansion, learning, and curiosity.
Saturn: Represents limitations, boundaries, responsibility, structure, and discipline.
Uranus: Governs unexpected events, change, innovation, creativity, and intuition.
Neptune: Rules over spirituality, psychic abilities, dreams, imagination, and the unconscious.
Pluto: Symbolizes transformation, power, regeneration, and the subconscious mind.

While the inner planets have a more direct influence on our daily lives and personalities, the outer planets govern deeper, more unconscious aspects of our existence, shaping our spiritual growth and collective consciousness.

Planets/Energy/Symobls

Zodiac	Planet	Houses
Aries ♈	Mars ♂	House 1
Taurus ♉	Venus ♀	House 2
Gemini ♊	Mercury ☿	House 3
Cancer ♋	Moon ☽	House 4
Leo ♌	Sun ☉	House 5
Virgo ♍	Mercury ☿	House 6
Libra ♎	Venus ♀	House 7
Scorpio ♏	Pluto ♇	House 8
Sagitttarius ♐	Jupiter ♃	House 9
Capricorn ♑	Saturn ♄	House 10
Aquarius ♒	Uranus ♅	House 11
Pisces ♓	Neptune ♆	House 12

Planets/Energy/Symobls

In astrology, the natal chart is divided into 12 houses, each representing a different area of life, akin to slices of a pizza. These houses are determined based on the position of celestial bodies at the time of your birth. The chart revolves around the Earth, with the horizon acting as a dividing line between the light and dark halves of the chart.

Each house corresponds to a specific aspect of life and is numbered starting from below the horizon line, moving counterclockwise around the chart. Just as each zodiac sign has a planetary ruler, each house also has a planetary and zodiac sign association. These associations help in understanding the influences on each house, although they can vary depending on the location of planets and signs in your natal chart.

For instance, Aries rules the first house, impacting that area of life, but its influence also extends to the sign occupying your first house in your natal chart. Similarly, Mars governs the first house but shifts based on the time of your birth, affecting different areas of your life accordingly.

To utilize astrology in magical rituals effectively, it's crucial to have your natal chart created, which reveals the precise locations of planets and signs in the houses at the time of your birth. This personalized chart provides insights into how celestial energies influence your life and guides your magical practices accordingly.

Planets/Energy/Symobls

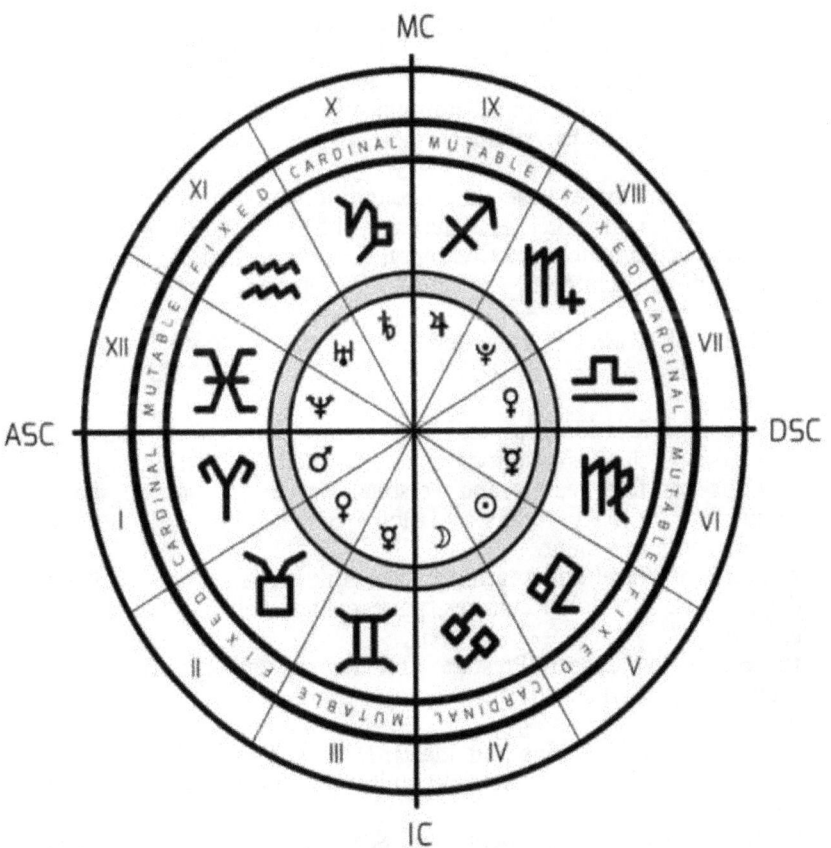

Astrological Houses

In astrology, the natal chart is divided into 12 houses, each representing different aspects of life.

1. **House of the Self:** Represents the individual's identity, personality, appearance, and how they project themselves to the world.
2. **House of Material Values and Security:** Deals with finances, possessions, material resources, and sense of security.
3. **House of Learning and Communication:** Focuses on education, communication skills, siblings, short trips, and local community interactions.
4. **House of Home Base and Grounding:** Pertains to the home environment, family life, roots, heritage, and emotional foundation.
5. **House of Romance and Creativity:** Governs love affairs, romantic relationships, children, creative expression, hobbies, and entertainment.
6. **House of Work Life and Health:** Deals with daily work routines, employment, service to others, health, wellness, and self-care practices.
7. **House of Relationships and Partnerships:** Represents marriage, partnerships, close associations, contracts, and legal matters.
8. **House of Life Secrets and Personal Needs:** Focuses on shared resources, intimacy, transformation, psychological depth, and personal empowerment.
9. **House of Travel and Learning:** Relates to higher education, long-distance travel, foreign cultures, philosophical beliefs, and spiritual growth.
10. **House of Career Prestige and Reputation:** Governs career aspirations, social status, public image, achievements, and authority figures.
11. **House of Friendships and Ideals:** Deals with friendships, social networks, group affiliations, humanitarian causes, and long-term goals.
12. **House of Intuition, Psychic, and Secrets:** Pertains to spirituality, intuition, psychic abilities, hidden enemies, subconscious mind, and solitude.

Understanding the significance of each house in the natal chart can provide valuable insights into various areas of life and guide personal growth, decision-making, and spiritual development.

The Moon

In the Northern Hemisphere the moon moves clockwise through the phases

In the Southern Hemisphere the moon moves counterclockwise.

Phases of the moon as seen in the Northern Hemisphere

| New | Waxing Crescent | Waxing Quarter | Waxing Gibbous | Full | Waning Gibbous | Waning Quarter | Waning Crescent | Dark Moon |

Phases of the moon as seen in the Southern Hemisphere

| New | Waxing Crescent | Waxing Quarter | Waxing Gibbous | Full | Waning Gibbous | Waning Quarter | Waning Crescent | Dark Moon |

Astrological Moon Correspondances

Here are the correspondences for each Moon sign in astrology:

Aries Moon: Associated with new beginnings, energy, and innovative ideas.

Taurus Moon: Brings grounding energy, focusing on love, financial stability, and success.

Gemini Moon: Facilitates communication, writing, and travel, encouraging intellectual curiosity.

Cancer Moon: Reflects female energy, emotions, and the home environment, nurturing and intuitive.

Leo Moon: Instills confidence, assertiveness, and a desire for recognition and leadership.

Virgo Moon: Emphasizes attention to detail, organization, and education, promoting practicality and service.

Libra Moon: Brings balance, harmony, and a sense of justice, fostering relationships and diplomacy.

Scorpio Moon: Encourages transformation, psychic growth, and delving into the depths of emotions.

Sagittarius Moon: Inspires truth-seeking, exploration, and pursuits related to law, philosophy, and publishing.

Capricorn Moon: Focuses on career, ambition, and striving for recognition and success in the public sphere.

Aquarius Moon: Promotes freedom, innovation, and creativity, emphasizing unconventional solutions.

Pisces Moon: Facilitates healing, intuition, clairvoyance, and accessing the realm of dreams and spirituality.

Moon Magic

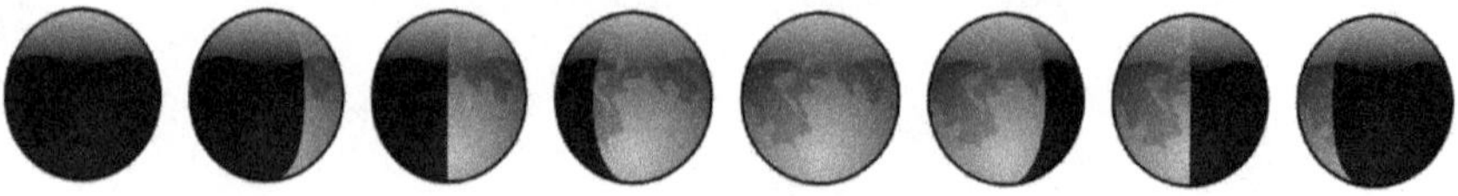

- **Waxing Gibbous**
  Pause
  Observe

- **Full Moon**
  Take Chances
  All Spells

- **First Quarter**
  Love Spells
  Luck Spells
  Healing

- **Waning Gibbous**
  Banishing Spells
  Protection Spells
  Cleanse & Dextox

- **Last Quarter**
  Rest
  Justice Spells

- **Waxing Crecent**
  Money Spells
  Career Spells
  Moon Water

- **Waning Crecent**
  Look Back
  Be Greatful

- **New Moon**
  Set Goals
  Prepare Alter

Moon Water

Moon water is regular water that has been blessed under the Moon. You can make it on any lunar phase (not just the Full Moon), while embracing this spell.

Ingredients:

*Drinking Water
*A clear bowl or container of any size

1. Pour water into your clear container.

2. Put the bowl in a safe place where it will be lit by moonlight. This could be outside or near a window inside your home. Transparent containers allow light to reach the water without obstructions. It's okay if its cloudy outside, moonlight (just like sunlight) can pierce through clouds easily.

3. Place the water in the moonlight and charge it with your energy.

"Moon above, thank you for this sacred water. It's already helped me with (Say your intentions here, as if you already have what you desire)."

Your intention could be anything you desire, attracting money, healing, relationships, etc.

4. While moon water doesn't have to be outside all night, make sure to collect it before dawn. Don't let the sunlight touch it.

5. Filter out any insects or dirt if you left it outside. Then store in a bottle or jar and a dark place until you use it.

Moon Water – Common Uses

Enhance Meditations

Being aware of your intuitive powers is key to realizing your full potential while meditating.

1. Light a blue or purple candle on your alter
2. Apply a drop of Moon Water to your Third Eye chakra (between your eyebrows). This will help open yourself to the devine.
3. Follow a guided meditation
4. Lean into the peaceful place, allow visions to come to you with ease. It's okay if they don't happen right away. Practice helps.

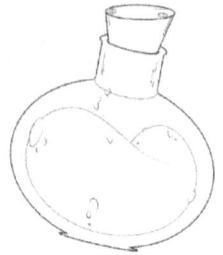

Finances

Want your money to flow like water? Have confidence that nothing can stop the flow of money into your life.

1. Bless your money by sprinkling just a few drops of Moon Water on your purse or wallet.
2. Visualize your intention and your future. Visualize the outcome you expect.

Home Cleansing

1. Clean your home as you normally would.
2. Sprinkle Moon Water with your fingers or a spray bottle wherever you want to bless.
3. Consider adding essential oils or herbs to infuse your positive energy.

Moon Water Baths

1. Fill bathtub and add some Moon Water. Climb in the tub and pour Moon Water on yourself.
2. Focus on the intention you've charged your Moon Water with. Focus on absorbing the light of that intent. Wash your hair with Moon Water to encuarge growth with a divine glow

Consecrate Crystals

Gemstones and crystals can be used to store, abosorb, and amplify energy.

1. Place stones outside under the Moon.
2. Place bowl of water next to them. (Make sure it's safe to wash your stones with water) then phisically clean them with Moon Water.

Moon Water Spells

Moon Water Spells

Moon Water Spells

Moon Water Spells

Sabbats and Esbats

Wheel of The Year

The Wheel of the Year symbolizes the Pagan seasonal cycle, comprised of eight festivals called Sabbats. It serves as a metaphor for the natural progression of seasons, mirroring the stages of birth, life, aging, and death within our own existence.

Sabbats

Samhain
Northern Hemispher October 31
Southern Hemispher April 30/May 1

Yule
Northern Hemispher December 21
Southern Hemispher June 20-23

Ostara
Northern Hemispher March 21
Southern Hemispher September 20-23

Beltane
Northern Hemisphere May 1
Southern Hemispher October 31

Litha
Northern Hemisphere June 21
Southern Hemispher December 20-23

Lughnasdh
Northern Hemisphere February 2
Southern Hemispher September 21

Mabon
Northern Hemisphere September 21
Southern Hemispher March 20-23

Also known as All Hallow's Eve or Halloween

Symbols: acorns, apples, autumn flowers, bat, black cats, bones, corn, crows, death & dying.

Colors: black, orange, red.

Crystals: beryl, opal, tourmaline, turquoise.

Essential Oils: cinnamon, myrrh, olive, patchouli.

Food: apples, cider, mulled cider, nuts, pork, pomegranates, potatoes, pumpkins, spices.

Goddess, Gods and Deities: Astarte, Belili, Demeter, Hathor, Ishtar, Kore, Lakshmi.

Herbs: almond, apple leaf, autumn joy, bay leaf, calendula, cinnamon, cloves, garlic, ginger, hazelnut, hemlock cones, mandrake root, marigold, sedum.

Incense: benzoin, copal, mastic resin, mugwort, myrrh, patchouli, sage, sandalwood, sweetgrass, wormwood.

Animals: crow, elephant, heron, jackal, raven, ram, robin, scorpion, stag.

The Pagan calendar commences and concludes with Samhain, marking a period of transformation and the eternal cycle of life. It's a moment for introspection, a time to look back on the year gone by. During Samhain night, the spiritual connection intensifies, and the veil between the living and the deceased thins, presenting both a potent and perilous opportunity to commune with departed loved ones. As darkness envelops, the Goddess assumes her role as the Crone, while the God descends into the underworld, preparing for rebirth alongside the Goddess at Yule. It's a juncture to contemplate and express gratitude for the time spent with those who have passed on.

Samhain

Yule
Also known as Winter Solstice

Symbols: rebirth of the Sun, the longest night of the year, & planning for future.

Colors: gold, green, red, silver, & white.

Crystals: bloodstone, clear quartz, dimond, emerald, garnet, & ruby.

Essential Oils: pine, frankincense, sweet orange, cypress, juniper, & clove.

Food: cookies, fruits, nuts, pork dishes, turkey, eggnog, ginger, teas, & spiced cider.

Goddess, Gods and Deities: Aphrodite, Fortuna, Gaia, Hel, HOlle, Ishtar, & Isis.

Herbs: bayberry, thistle, evergreen, frankincense, holly, laurel, mistletow, oak, pine, sage & yellow cedar.

Incense: cedar, frakincense, juniper, myrrh, & pine.

Animals: crow, elephant, heron, jackal, raven, ram, robin, scorpion, stag.

Yule marks the Winter Solstice, the shortest day and longest night of the year, signifying the Earth's transition towards longer days and the gradual return of warmth with the resurgence of the Sun. This festive occasion entails candlelit gatherings, lavish feasts, and adornments of greenery to herald the imminent arrival of Spring. Traditionally, Yule logs, hewn from hardwood trees, are ceremonially burned, dwindling to a small remnant saved to kindle the following year's Yule fire. Inside homes, a decorated Yule Tree, often adorned with a pentagram atop symbolizing the five elements, stands as a centerpiece. Many practitioners, remaining awake through the night, eagerly await the Sun's return, while exchanging gifts adds to the joyous atmosphere.

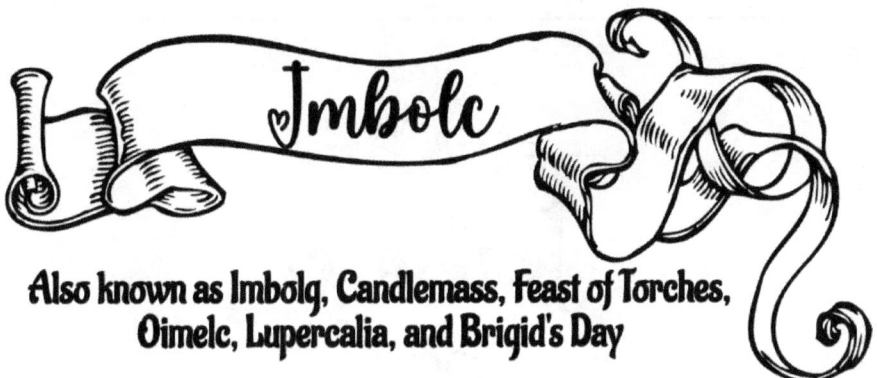

Imbolc

Also known as Imbolg, Candlemass, Feast of Torches, Oimelc, Lupercalia, and Brigid's Day

Symbols: growth, renewal, reunion, dispensing of the old and clearing way for the new.

Colors: white, pink, red, yellow, light green, & brown.

Crystals: amethyst, bloodstone, garnet, ruby, onyx, turquoise.

Essential Oils: cinnamon, cedarwood, lavendar, lemon, rosemary, jasmine, & rose.

Food: pumpkin, sunflower, poppyseed cakes, muffins, scones, dairy products, peppers, onions, garlic, and raisins.

Goddess, Gods and Deities: Brighid, Aradia, Athena, Inanna, Gaia, Februa, Aengus Og, Eros, & Feruus.

Herbs: angelica, basil, bay laurel, blackberry, celandine, coltsfoot, heather, iris, myrrh, snowdrops, tansy, & violets

Incense: basil, frankincense, myrrh, wisteria, jasmine, camphor, cinnamon, & lotus.

Animals: wolf, snake, swan, vulture, robin, burrowing animals, sheep, lamb, & deer.

Imbolc heralds a period of fresh starts and contemplation of the year ahead. Recognizable by the emergence of the first green shoots of Spring, it encourages reflection on new beginnings and pays homage to
the nurturing essence of femininity. It's a moment to prepare for the imminent arrival of Spring, embracing the promise of growth and renewal.

Imbolc

Also known as Eostre, Spring/Vernal Equinox

Symbols: Hope, renewal, growth, return of the light, hearth and home, and purification.

Colors: white, pink, red, yellow, light green, and brown.

Crystals: amethyst, bloodstone, garnet, ruby, onyx, turquoise.

Essential Oils: cinnamon, cedarwood, lavendar, lemon, rosemary, jasmine, & rose.

Food: pumpkin, sunflower, poppyseed cakes, muffins, scones, dairy products, peppers, onions, garlic, and raisins.

Goddess, Gods and Deities: Brighid, Aradia, Athena, Inanna, Gaia, Februa, Aengus Og, Eros, & Feruus.

Herbs: angelica, basil, bay laurel, blackberry, celandine, coltsfoot, heather, iris, myrrh, snowdrops, tansy, & violets

Incense: basil, frankincense, myrrh, wisteria, jasmine, camphor, cinnamon, & lotus.

Animals: wolf, snake, swan, vulture, robin, burrowing animals, sheep, lamb, & deer.

The equinoxes mark the equilibrium within the seasonal cycle, where day and night share equal lengths. This Sabbat signifies the Earth's rejuvenation as daylight extends. Witches honor new life, portraying it through symbols of buds, blossoms, leaves, and eggs. It's a period ripe for creative endeavors and active engagement with life. Depictions of Ostara evoke themes of childhood and beginnings. It's an occasion to joyfully celebrate the precious gift of life.

Ostara

Beltane

Also known as Bealtaine, Walpurgisnach, May Day, Novey Eve

Symbols: Celebration of fertility, May Pole, Great Rite, eggs, butterchurns, fresh flowers, and chalices.

Colors: red, white, pink, brown, and green

Crystals: asparkling citrines, clear crystal quartz, golden tiger's eye, amber, and topaz.

Essential Oils: geranium, ylang ylang, jasmine, and frankincense.

Food: dairy, oatmeal, cakes, bread, cherries, strawberries, green salads

Goddess, Gods and Deities: All Flower Goddesses, Maeve, Tanit, Flora, Maia, Danu, Luna, Guinevere, and Gaid.

Herbs: primrose, yellow cowslip, roses, lily of the valley, honeysuckle, birtch trees, rosemary, lilac, angelica, ash trees, bluebells, cinquefoil, daisies, frankincense, ivy marigold.

Incense: basil, frankincense, myrrh, wisteria, jasmine, camphor, cinnamon, & lotus.

Animals: wolf, snake, swan, vulture, robin, burrowing animals, sheep, lamb, & deer.

Beltane, marking the onset of the Summer season, falls at a cross-quarter point and commemorates the Great Rite and the sacred union of sexuality. This spring fertility festival is characterized by feasting, jubilation, and a celebration of love, making it an especially cherished time for lovers. In Wiccan tradition, Beltane holds particular significance as it's the favored season for witches to partake in handfasting ceremonies.

Also known as Summer Solstice, Midsummer

Symbols: fire, the Sun, blades, mistletoe, oak trees, balefires, sun wheels, sunflowers, summer fruites, seashells, and faeries.

Colors: gold, red, orange, blue, yellow and green.

Crystals: amber, tiger's eye, jade, emerald.

Essential Oils: lavender, rosemary, and pine.

Food: peppers, onions, asparagus, honey, fresh vegetables, red wine, straberries, herbal teas, citrus fruit, summer squash, salads, and herbs such as basil, fennel, & lavender.

Goddess, Gods and Deities: Aine, Freya, Flora, Habondia, Lugh, Greenman, Oak King, Bast, Brigit, and Hathor.

Herbs: mugwort, vervain, chamomile, rose, honeysuckle, lily, oak, lavendar, ivy, yarrow, fern, elder, wild thyme, daisy, and carnation.

Incense: sage, cedar, frankincense, lemon, myrrh, pine, rose, and lavender.

Animals: butterfly, bee, wren, robin, and snake.

Litha, observed during the Summer Solstice, commemorates the longest day of the year when nature's energies reach their peak. Traditionally, the vigor and brilliance of summer were honored through bonfires and staying awake throughout the brief night. A customary practice involved leaping over the bonfire as a means of ensuring a bountiful harvest, adding to the festive spirit of the occasion.

Lammas

Also known as Lughnasadh or Lunasa

Symbols: harvesting of grain, fruitfullness, reaping, prosperity, reverence, purification, transformation, change, The Bread of Life, The Chalice of Plenty, and The Ever-flowing Cup.

Colors: orange, gold, yellow, and purple.

Crystals: yellow diamonds, aventurine, peridot, and citrine.

Essential Oils: Lavendar, lemongrass, and patchouli.

Food: bread, corn, potatoes, berry pies, barley cakes, nuts, berries, apples, rice, roast lamb, acorns, apples, oats, grains, elderberry wine, ale, and meadowsweet tea.

Goddess, Gods and Deities: Aine, Ceres, Cerridwen, Demeter, Inanna, Ishtar, Kore, Persphone, Adonis, Dumuzi, Lugh, Odin, Loki, and Baal.

Herbs: acacia flowers, aloes, calendula, cornstalks, cyclamen, fenugreek, frankincense, heather, hollyhock, myrtle, oak leaves, sunflower, and vervain.

Incense: aloes, rose, rose hips, rosemary, chamomile, passionflower, frankincense, and sandalwood.

Animals: roosters, calves, and stags.

Lammas, a cross-quarter day, signifies the harvest of the first grain. During the celebration, the initial loaf of bread made from this grain is ceremonially broken and shared in honor of the Goddess. This Sabbat embodies the theme of confronting change and the challenges it presents.

Also known as Autumn Equinx and Madron

Symbols: wine, gourds, pine cones, acornes, grains, corn, apples, pomegranates, vines, ivy, dried seeds, and horns of pleanty.

Colors: brown, red, maroon, orange, yellow, and gold.

Crystals: amber, amethyst, citrine, topaz, and tiger-eye.

Essential Oils: clove, frankincense, and ceader wood.

Food: breads, nuts, apples, pomegranates, and vegtables like patatoes, carrots, and onions.

Goddess, Gods and Deities: Arawn, Ashtoreth, Ceridwen, Demeter, Persephone, Epona, Freya, Hathor, Inanna, Istar, Isis, Kore, Modrun, Morrigan, Venus, Bacchus, Cernunnos, Dagda, and Thoth.

Herbs: acorn, benzoin, ferns, grains, honeysuckle, marigold, milkweed, myrrh, passionflower, rose, sage, tobacco, thistle, and vegetables.

Incense: benzion, cedar, frankincense, myrrh, and pine.

Animals: blackbird, butterfly, dog, eagle, hawk, owl, pig, salmon, snake, stag, swallow, Swan, turkey vulture, wolf.

This Sabbat, known for its equal hours of day and night, represents the balance between light and dark. It marks the celebration of the second harvest, where food is meticulously prepared, preserved, and stored for the impending winter. This joyous occasion is a tribute to the bountiful harvest and the abundance it brings, emphasizing themes of home and family. It's also an opportune moment for witches to reflect on their craft, reaffirming their dedication to celebrating magic and ritual.

Mabon

The Esbats

There are eight main Sabbats that correspond to the seasons and harvest times, celebrated during the day and focusing on masculine energy. Most modern Witches and Pagans observe these Sabbats along with a regular Esbat every year.

In contrast, Esbats revolve around the cycles of the Moon, serving as a time for performing magick and honoring appropriate deities. Whether part of a coven or practicing solo, Esbats are typically celebrated during the Full Moon. The phases of the moon impact various aspects of our lives, with most Witches following standard Moon phases such as New Moon, Crescent, First Quarter, Full Moon, Last Quarter, and Dark Moon.

The Esbats

Each Moon phase signifies different types of magickal work. For instance, setting intentions and goals aligns with the New Moon, while banishing and releasing correspond to the period from Full Moon to Dark Moon.

This section focuses on celebrating the Full Monthly Moons, each with its unique meaning and magickal purpose. Additionally, the Full Moon serves as a traditional time for divination practices, benefiting from the Moon's potent energy.

As you delve into Witchcraft, you'll encounter various associations with gods, goddesses, rocks, herbs, and colors linked to each monthly Moon. While traditions differ, it's essential to find what resonates with you. Recognizing that Wicca originated in the Northern Hemisphere, those in the Southern Hemisphere may need to adapt practices to align with their seasons and experiences, emphasizing the importance of individualized approaches to spiritual connection.

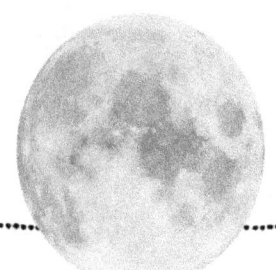

The Esbats

**Monthly Moons
Northern & Southern Hemispher counterparts:**

January
Wolf Moon - Mead Moon
February
Snow Moon - Corn Moon
March
Worm Moon - Harvest Moon
April
Pink Moon - Seed Moon
May
Flower Moon - Hare Moon
June
Strawberry Moon - Oak Moon
July
Buck Moon - Wolf Moon
August
Sturgeon Moon - Storm Moon
September
Harvest Moon - Worm Moon
October
Hunter's Moon - Seed Moon
November
Beaver Moon - Hare Moon
December
Cold Moon - Honey Moon

Wolf Moon

During the Wolf Moon, also known as the Cold Snow or Winter Moon, we seek protection for our home and family. This moon phase represents strength and resilience, particularly during the winter season when we may face challenges. As we embrace the energy of this moon, we recognizeits significance in marking both endings and beginnings. It's a time for reflection, rest, and planning for the renewal of spring.

Here are some correspondences associated with the Wolf Moon:

Month: January (Northern Hemisphere) / July (Southern Hemisphere)
Element: Air
Zodiac: Capricorn, Aquarius (Northern Hemisphere) / Cancer, Leo (Southern Hemisphere)
Symbols: Wolves, courage, hunting
Colors: Black, white, silver
Goddesses, Gods, and Deities: Inanna, Freyja
Crystals: Hematite, amethyst, garnet
Incense: Angelica, African violet, cedarwood
Herbs: Thistle, nuts, seeds, marjoram
Essential Oils: Musk, mimosa
Animals: Fox, coyote, pheasant

During this time, we ask for protection and strength to safeguard our homes and loved ones against any challenges or adversities that may come our way. Let us embrace the energy of the Wolf Moon and harness its power for our well-being and security.

Storm Moon

During the Storm Moon, also known as the Death or Quickening Moon, we seek guidance from spirit in planning our future. This moon phase signifies a time of focusing on our health, fertility, and inner strength. As we transition from the winter season, characterized by storms and short days, we reflect on the challenges we face in life and how to overcome them.

Here are some correspondences associated with the Storm Moon:

Month: February (Northern Hemisphere) / August (Southern Hemisphere)
Element: Fire
Zodiac: Aquarius, Pisces (Northern Hemisphere) / Leo, Virgo (Southern Hemisphere)
Symbols: Heavy snowing, bones, hunger
Colors: Purple and blue
Goddesses, Gods, and Deities: Brighid, Aphrodite, Juno, Mars
Crystals: Rose quartz, jasper, amethyst
Incense: Allspice, rose geranium, lemongrass
Herbs: Hyssop, sage, myrrh
Essential Oils: Musk, mimosa
Animals: Otter, unicorn, eagle

During this time, we call upon spirit for assistance in navigating our path forward. May we find the strength and wisdom to overcome challengesand embrace the opportunities for growth and renewal that lie ahead.

Worm Moon

The Worm Moon, also known as the Chaste or Seed Moon, is a time associated with planting seeds or fostering ideas of positivity, success, and hope for the future. As the beginning of Spring symbolizes purity and new beginnings, it's an opportune moment to mentally prepare
oneself for new experiences that may soon enter their life.

Here are some correspondences associated with the Storm Moon:

Month: March (Northern Hemisphere) / September (Southern Hemisphere)
Element: Water
Zodiac: Pisces, Aries (Northern Hemisphere) / Virgo, Libra (Southern Hemisphere)
Symbols: Worms, robins, maple
Colors: Green, yellow, purple
Goddesses, Gods, and Deities: Isis, the Morrighan, Artemis, Cybele
Crystals: Bloodstone, aquamarine
Incense: Cedarwood, allspice
Herbs: High John, pennyroyal, wood betony, apple blossom
Essential Oils: Honeysuckle, apple blossom
Animals: Cougar, hedgehog, boar, crow, eagle

Seed Moon

To consult the Moon for guidance and plant the seeds of your dreams, consider the following correspondences for the Seed Moon:

The Seed Moon, also known as the Egg, Grass, or Wind Moon, ushers in a period of fertility, growth, and wisdom. It signifies a transition from planting ideas to taking action towards realizing your dreams. Embrace confidence and take proactive steps to pursue your goals. Trust in yourself and your abilities to manifest your aspirations.

Here are some correspondences associated with the Storm Moon:

Month: April (Northern Hemisphere) / October (Southern Hemisphere)
Element: Air
Zodiac: Aries, Taurus (Northern Hemisphere) / Libra, Scorpio (Southern Hemisphere)
Symbols: Pink moss, spring eggs
Colors: Red, yellow, blue
Goddesses, Gods, and Deities: Ishtar, Tawaret, Venus, Herne, Cernunnos
Crystals: Quartz, selenite, angelite
Incense: Ambergris, jasmine, rose, rosemary
Herbs: Dandelion, milkweed, dogwood, fennel, dill
Essential Oils: Pine, bay, bergamot, patchouli

Use these correspondences to attune yourself with the energies of the Seed Moon and take bold steps towards manifesting your dreams and goals.

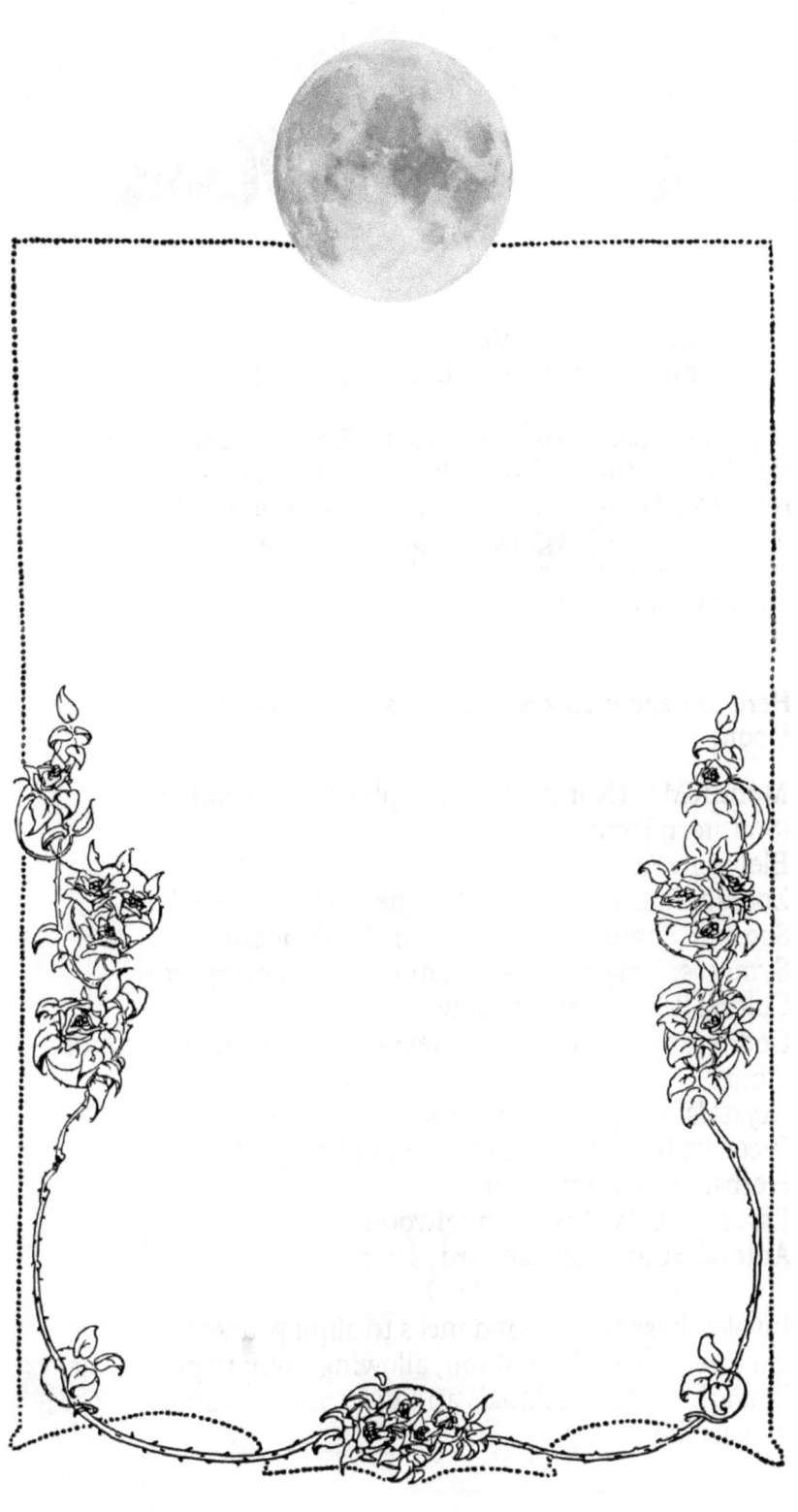

Hare Moon

Seek guidance from the Moon and reaffirm your goals, consider the correspondences for the Hare Moon:

The Hare Moon, also known as the Flower or Planting Moon, signifies a time of health, wisdom, success, love, and romance. As you witness your efforts blooming and coming to fruition, you'll begin to see positive changes manifesting in your life, even if they are gradual. Use this time to rekindle the romantic spark in your relationship, fostering deeper connections and intimacy.

Here are some correspondences associated with the Storm Moon:

Month: May (Northern Hemisphere) / November (Southern Hemisphere)
Element: Fire
Zodiac: Taurus, Gemini (Northern Hemisphere) / Scorpio, Sagittarius (Southern Hemisphere)
Symbols: Flowers, fertility, mothers, planting, corn
Colors: Red, orange, yellow
Goddesses, Gods, and **Deities:** Kali, Priapus, Cernunnos, Flora
Crystals: Ruby, garnet, amber, apache tear
Incense: Basil, bergamot, cardamom, cypress
Herbs: Mint, cinnamon
Essential Oils: Rose, sandalwood
Animals: Cat, lynx, leopard, swan

Invoke these correspondences to align yourself with the energies of the Hare Moon, allowing them to guide you in reaffirming your goals and fostering positive changes in your life.

Honey Moon

The Moon can indeed assist in balancing spiritual and physical needs. Here are the correspondences for the Honey Moon:

The Honey Moon, also known as the Lovers, Strawberry, or Rose Moon, carries energies of love, romance, and partnerships. It's a time to nurture relationships and reflect on the positive aspects of life.

Here are some correspondences associated with the Storm Moon:

Month: June (Northern Hemisphere) / December (Southern Hemisphere)
Element: Earth
Zodiac: Gemini, Cancer (Northern Hemisphere) / Sagittarius, Capricorn (Southern Hemisphere)
Symbols: Strawberries, roses, honey, mead, summer
Colors: Gold, yellow, orange
Goddesses, Gods, and Deities: Isis, Cerridwen, Juno, Persephone
Crystals: Topaz, agate
Incense: Lavender, African violet
Herbs: Parsley, mosses, skullcap, mugwort
Essential Oils: Lily of the valley, lavender
Animals: Monkey, butterfly, frog, toad, peacock

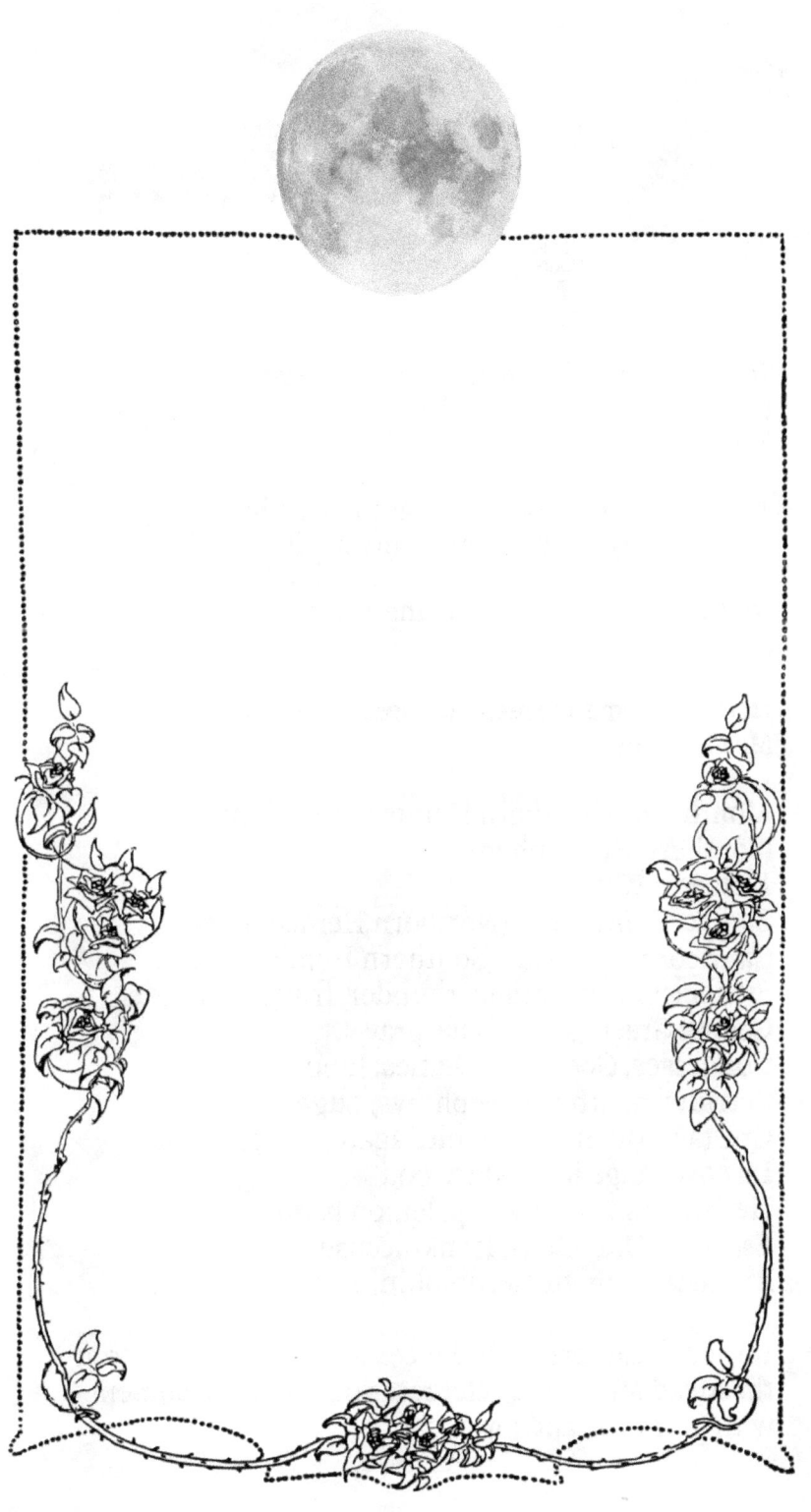

Mead Moon

To seek guidance from the Moon once your goals have been achieved, consider the correspondences for the Mead Moon:

The Mead Moon, also known as the Blessing, Thunder, or Lightning Moon, represents a time of rebirth, success, and strength. It marks the first harvest or the fruition of your labor, inviting you to celebrate your achievements.

Here are some correspondences associated with the Mead Moon:

Month: July (Northern Hemisphere) / January (Southern Hemisphere)
Element: Water
Zodiac: Cancer, Leo (Northern Hemisphere) / Capricorn, Aquarius (Southern Hemisphere)
Symbols: Buck, antlers, thunder, fruits, ripe corn
Colors: Green, silver, blue-gray
Goddesses, Gods, and Deities: Juno, Venus, Cerridwen, Athena, Nephthys, Lugh
Crystals: Moonstone, white agate, opals, pearls
Incense: Angelica, cedarwood
Herbs: Mugwort, hyssop, lemon balm
Essential Oils: Orris, frankincense
Animals: Crab, turtle, dolphin, whale, ibis

Invoke these correspondences to seek guidance from the Mead Moon and celebrate your accomplishments with gratitude and joy.

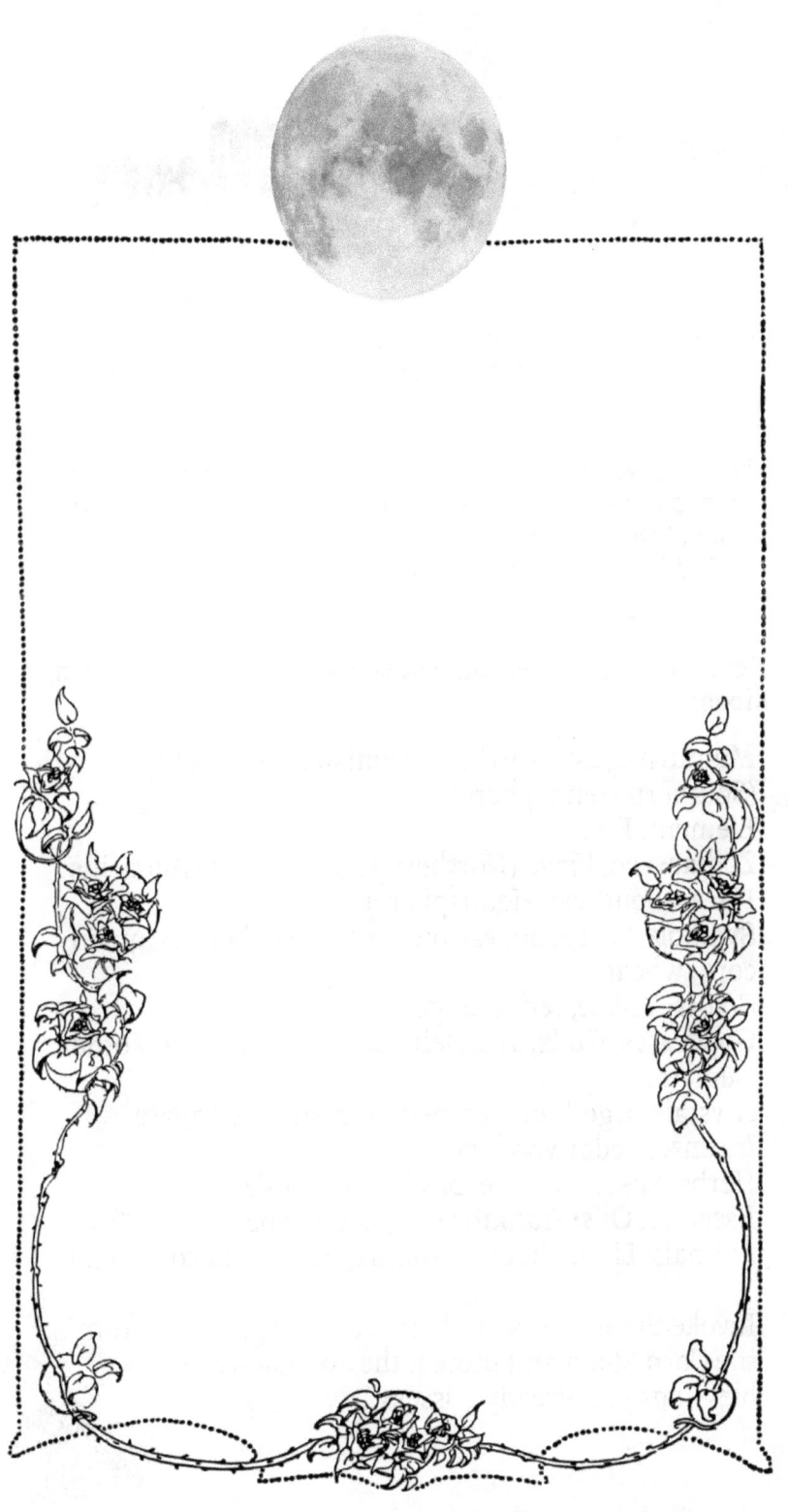

Corn Moon

To seek guidance from the Moon to protect what you already have, consider the correspondences for the Corn Moon:

The Corn Moon, also known as the Wyrt, Barley, or Red Moon, signifies a period of abundance and preparation for seasonal changes. It's essential to connect with the spirit of the Goddess to express gratitude for the abundance in your life and to assist others in reaching their full potential.

Here are some correspondences associated with the Corn Moon:

Month: August (Northern Hemisphere) / February (Southern Hemisphere)
Element: Fire
Zodiac: Leo, Virgo (Northern Hemisphere) / Aquarius, Pisces (Southern Hemisphere)
Symbols: Sturgeon, various fishes, blueberries, green corn, wheat
Colors: Yellow, red, orange
Goddesses, Gods, and Deities: Ceres, the Corn Mother, Demeter
Crystals: Tiger's eye, carnelian, garnet, red agate
Incense: Cedarwood, citron
Herbs: Rosemary, rue, basil, chamomile
Essential Oils: Frankincense, heliotrope
Animals: Lion, phoenix, sphinx, dragon, falcon, eagle

Invoke these correspondences to seek guidance from the Corn Moon and protect the abundance and blessings you already possess.

Harvest Moon

To connect with spirit through the Moon and express gratitude for all you have, consider the correspondences for the Harvest Moon:

The Harvest Moon, also known as the Barley or Hunters Moon, embodies energies of protection, prosperity, and abundance. It's a time to give thanks for all that you possess and to nurture others around you. Focus on your health, especially if you've been unwell, and be mindful of both your own energy and that of others.

Here are some correspondences associated with the Harvest Moon:

Month: September (Northern Hemisphere) / March (Southern Hemisphere)
Element: Earth
Zodiac: Virgo, Libra (Northern Hemisphere) / Pisces, Aries (Southern Hemisphere)
Symbols: Harvest, autumn, corn, barley, plums
Colors: Brown, green
Goddesses, Gods, and Deities: Demeter, Brighid, Freyja, Vesta
Crystals: Citrine, chrysolite, peridot, bloodstone
Incense: Amber, chamomile
Herbs: Wheat, valerian, witch hazel, skullcap
Essential Oils: Storax, mastic, gardenia, bergamot
Animals: Snake, jackal, ibis, sparrow

Invoke these correspondences to connect with the spirit through the Harvest Moon and express gratitude for the abundance and blessings in your life.

Blood Moon

To use the Moon to connect with those who have passed and remember them, consider the correspondences for the Blood Moon:

The Blood Moon, also known as the Falling Leaf or Hunters Moon, invites you to set new goals, be mindful of your spiritual grounding and protection, and engage in divination practices. As nature prepares for winter, it's a time to reflect on the past year and prepare for the one ahead.

Here are some correspondences associated with the Blood Moon:

Month: October (Northern Hemisphere) / April (Southern Hemisphere)
Element: Air
Zodiac: Libra, Scorpio (Northern Hemisphere) / Aries, Taurus (Southern Hemisphere)
Symbols: Hunting, travel, fallen leaves
Colors: Dark blue, black, purple
Goddesses, Gods, and Deities: Herne, Apollo, Cernunnos, Mercury
Crystals: Obsidian, amethyst, tourmaline
Incense: Mastic, myrrh
Herbs: Apple blossom, pennyroyal, mint, catnip, sweet annie
Essential Oils: Strawberry, apple blossom, cherry
Animals: Stag, jackal, elephant, ram, scorpion, heron, crow

Invoke these correspondences to connect with the energy of the Blood Moon and honor the memory of those who have passed, while also setting intentions for the future and engaging in spiritual practices.

Snow Moon

To use the Moon to rid yourself of negative thoughts and vibrations, consider the correspondences for the Snow Moon:

The Snow Moon, also known as the Beaver Moon or Tree Moon, encourages you to focus on strengthening family and friendship bonds, as well as abundance and prosperity. This is an excellent time to seek guidance for the year ahead through practices such as Tarot readings. Take steps to reduce stress and prioritize spending time with loved ones.

Here are some correspondences associated with the Snow Moon:

Month: November (Northern Hemisphere) / May (Southern Hemisphere)
Element: Water
Zodiac: Scorpio, Sagittarius (Northern Hemisphere) / Taurus, Gemini (Southern Hemisphere)
Symbols: Beavers, fur, frost
Colors: Black, white, purple
Goddesses, Gods, and Deities: Astarte, Cailleach, Cerridwen, Circe, Freyja, Hathor
Crystals: Topaz, obsidian, onyx, apache tear
Incense: Myrrh, pine, sage
Herbs: Ginger, hops, wormwood, hyssop
Essential Oils: Cedar, cherry blossoms, hyacinth, narcissus, peppermint, lemon
Animals: Unicorn, scorpion, crocodile, jackal, owl

Invoke these correspondences to utilize the energy of the Snow Moon to release negative thoughts and vibrations, and to foster positivity, abundance, and harmony in your life.

Oak Moon

To consult the Moon for guidance and strength to achieve your goals, consider the correspondences for the Oak Moon:

The Oak Moon, also known as the Cold or Long Night Moon, signifies a time of hope and healing. With more hours of the night than the day, it's a period for rest and recuperation. Use this time to complete tasks you've worked hard on and tie up loose ends. Embrace the opportunity to let go of old habits and start fresh with new goals and intentions. Release any negative influences from your life in preparation for the longer days ahead.

Here are some correspondences associated with the Oak Moon:

Month: December (Northern Hemisphere) / June (Southern Hemisphere)
Element: Fire
Zodiac: Sagittarius, Capricorn (Northern Hemisphere) / Gemini, Cancer (Southern Hemisphere)
Symbols: Winter, long night, ice
Colors: White, red, black
Goddesses, Gods, and Deities: Minerva, Osiris, Athena, Persephone, Hades
Crystals: Obsidian, ruby, serpentine
Incense: Patchouli, oakmoss
Herbs: Ivy, mistletoe, holly, berries, cinnamon
Essential Oils: Violet, patchouli, rose geranium, frankincense, myrrh, lilac
Animals: Unicorn, scorpion, crocodile, jackal, owl, sparrow

Invoke these correspondences to seek guidance and draw strength from the energy of the Oak Moon as you strive to achieve your goals and embark on a new journey of growth and renewal.

Witch's Tools

Altar:
An altar serves as the focal point for your rituals and worship, providing a space for concentration and mindfulness in your practice. It houses sacred tools, items for blessings and offerings, components for spells, and objects that aid in your rituals.

Athame:
The athame is a double-edged dagger utilized as a tool in rituals for directing energy and casting circles. While it resembles a dagger, it is not intended for physical cutting and serves as a substitute for a wand in magical workings.

Bell:
The bell, used for centuries to drive away evil spirits, creates vibrations that bring power and harmony to a magic circle. It can also signal the end of a ceremony or evoke the goddess.

Broom:
The broom, or besom, sweeps ceremonial areas before rituals, clearing out negative energies. Made with birch twigs, ash or oak wood, and willow wands, it symbolizes purification.

Boline:
A boline is a knife used for cutting items during rituals, serving as a practical tool for witches.

Witch's Tools

Book Of Shadows:
A Witch's notebook containing rituals, spells, correspondences, symbolism, and information about witchcraft rules, passed down or personalized by each practitioner.

Cakes and Ale:
An optional ceremony during Sabbats and Esbats, involving prepared symbolic food and drink, representing the good things in life.

Candle:
Used to symbolize deities or elements and to absorb and release energy during spell rituals, candles are integral to witchcraft, with different colors holding specific significance.

Cauldron:
Symbolizing the womb and associated with water, the cauldron represents life's beginnings and is used for rituals involving prophecy and magicalwork. Always use heat-protective bed such as sand when burning.

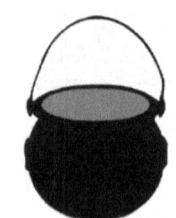

Chalice/Cup:
Representing water and used in conjunction with the athame in some rituals, the chalice can be passed among participants as a bonding ritual.

Crystals:
Chosen based on correspondences and intentions, crystals enhance the energy of rituals and spells and can include birthstones for added significance.

Witch's Tools

Decorations/Divination Tools:
Any item used in rituals serves as a tool, with no fixed rules on setup.
Intuition guides choices, allowing personalization of the altar.

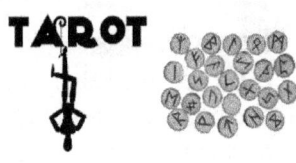

Goddesses/Gods/Deities
Understanding and respecting the power of deities is crucial before invoking them in rituals, with emphasis on both feminine and masculine energies.

Herbs
Beneficial for physical and spiritual well-being, herbs are incorporated into witchcraft rituals based on their properties and correspondences.

Incense/Censer:
Used to create a sacred atmosphere and connection with Spirit, incense represents the element of air and is integral to ritual and magical workings.

Libations:
Pouring liquid or grains as offerings to deities, libations can be part of rituals and ceremonies.

Oils/Aromatherapy:
Supplementing spells and rituals, oils enhance magical properties and can be used for anointing tools, talismans, or the body.

Witch's Tools

Pentacle:
A protective talisman representing earth, the pentacle holds items used in rituals and ceremonies and is sometimes worn as jewelry.

Robes/Cloak:
Special robes worn during ceremonies serve as a way to step into the magical world, with styles and colors often dictated by tradition or group practices.

Salt:
Used to represent earth and water, salt holds magical significance and is associated with protection and purification.

Tarot
Though not directly related to witchcraft, Tarot cards are valuable tools for reflection and guidance, connecting with universal energies.

Wand:
Used to direct energy and symbolize male energy and power, wands can consecrate spaces and invoke deities, traditionally made of wood with various magical associations.

Water:
Essential for life and associated with emotions and the Moon, water represents cleansing, healing, and nourishment in rituals and ceremonies.

Magical Timing

Sunday Magic

Leadership, Money, Power, Health, Fatherhood, Vitality, Happiness

Embrace the radiant energy of Sunday, a day that resonates with the vibrant power of the sun, a celestial beacon of light. Overflowing with potential for success, wealth, and recognition, Sundays offer a golden opportunity to pursue personal triumphs and bask in the glow of achievement.
Harness the enchanting potential of Sunday with these captivating rituals:

Welcome the dawn with reverence, invoking the radiant presence of the goddess Brigid for guidance and inspiration.
Adorn yourself with gleaming gold jewelry or don attire in hues of sunshine yellow, inviting the transformative magic of color into your life.

Elevate your surroundings with the vibrant presence of sunflowers, imbuing them with the essence of fame and ambition.
Scatter the petals of marigolds, symbols of prosperity, to invite abundance and financial blessings into your life.

Indulge in baked goods such as cinnamon rolls, infusing each delightful bite with intentions of health and success for yourself and your loved ones.

Savor the sweetness of oranges, nature's solar fruit, and feel the surge of magical energy infusing your vitality and happiness.

On Sundays, seize the opportunity to cultivate leadership, prosperity, and well-being as you align yourself with the radiant energies of the sun.

Monday Magic

Mothers, Nurturing Fertility, Growth, Clarity, Beauty, and Divination

Monday is a day dedicated to the mystical and mesmerizing energies of the moon. As the celestial guardian of women's mysteries, illusion, and prophetic dreaming, Mondays offer a gateway to delve into the depths of emotions, embark on journeys, and nurture fertility.

Unlock the magic of Monday with these captivating rituals:

Infuse your silver jewelry with the moon's radiant energy by exposing them to her light. Adorn yourself with moonstone or pearl jewelry, adorning your attire with lunar shimmer and subtle elegance in shades of white, silver, and blue.

Craft spells for safe travels using the mystical energy of a simple moonstone, ensuring protection and guidance on your journeys.

Embrace the floral companionship of bluebells, jasmine, gardenias, or white roses, weaving a tapestry of garden witchery infused with the moon's essence.

Channel the lunar wisdom of the Tarot, setting up a sacred space to enhance your psychic powers and intuition.

Nourish your body and soul with the serene energy of lunar fruits such as melons, promoting health, serenity, and inner peace.

Brew a soothing cup of chamomile or mint tea, imbuing it with intentions for sweet dreams and restful sleep, allowing the moon's gentle embrace to guide you into realms of tranquility.

Tuesday Magic

Courage, Success, Lust, Competition, Conflict, Survival, Money, and Leadership.

Embrace the fiery energy of Tuesday, a day ruled by Mars, the god of war. Strength and courage reign supreme. As the day for rebels and warriors, Tuesdays beckon you to harness the power of magic to bolster your resolve and ignite your passions.

Ignite your inner fire with these potent enchantments:

Embrace the vibrant hues of scarlet, red, black, and orange, infusing your attire with the bold and bewitching colors of Mars. Let your wardrobe exude confidence and command attention as you stride through the day.

Carry a bloodstone in your pocket or adorn yourself with garnet-studded jewelry, invoking the protective energies of these stones to fortify your convictions and embolden your spirit.

Commune with protective and fire-associated plants such as the snapdragon, thistle, and holly, weaving their potent energies into your shields and enhancing your bravery in the face of adversity.

Illuminate your surroundings with the fiery glow of spicy-scented candles, infusing your home with magical aromatherapy to invigorate your senses and amplify your energy.

Indulge in a hearty meal featuring Mars-aligned foods such as carrots, peppers, and garlic, infusing each bite with the power of victory and success. Let the nourishing flavors fuel your determination and propel you towards triumph.

On Tuesdays, embrace your inner warrior and tap into the potent energies of Mars to conquer challenges, ignite your passions, and emerge victorious in all your endeavors.

Wednesday Magic

Communication, Self Expression, Art, Wisdom. Addiction, and Divination.

Wednesday, is a day ruled by Mercury, the messenger god, where communication, change, and creativity collide in a whirlwind of excitement. Just like its patron deity, Wednesdays are filled with contradictions and surprises, offering endless opportunities for transformation and cunning endeavors.

Here are some enchanting ideas to infuse your Wednesday with magic:

Infuse your day with Wednesday's vibrant energies by adorning yourself in hues of purple or orange, invoking the colors associated with this dynamic day.

Carry a multi-purpose agate with you throughout the day, tapping into its versatile charms to adapt to any situation and seize opportunities for change.

Work with magical plants like the fern for protection and enhancement of other magical endeavors, amplifying their power and potency.

Incorporate the soothing scent of lavender into your charms and spells to facilitate transformation and embrace the winds of change.

Harness the enchanting aroma of lily of the valley to enhance your memory or commune with the spirit of the aspen tree for enhanced communication skills.

Channel your creativity through a Tarot spell, fanning out the cards to unlock new insights and unleash your artistic potential.

Thursday Magic

Growth, Expansion, Prosperity, Abundance, Success, Health, Business

Embrace the abundant energies of Thursday, ruled by Jupiter, the planet of prosperity and good health. Known as "Thor's day," this Norse god lends his strength and abundance to this auspicious day. Here are some enchanting ideas to enhance your Thursday:

Adorn yourself in regal shades of blue, purple, or green to align with the majestic energies of Jupiter. Notice how these colors uplift your mood and amplify your magical intentions.

Carry a turquoise tumbled stone in your pocket to attract protective and healing energies into your life, fostering abundance and well-being.

Incorporate honeysuckle blossoms and cinquefoil foliage into prosperity charms, invoking the lush abundance associated with these magical plants.

Call upon Thor for strength and abundance, or invoke the Roman god Jupiter for peace and wisdom in resolving conflicts.

Enhance your charms with sacred oak leaves, symbols of strength and resilience revered by Thor and Jupiter, to amplify the potency of your spells.

Bake a loaf of whole wheat bread and imbue it with blessings for abundance and gratitude. Offer thanks to the gods for your family and the gift of good health that sustains you.

On Thursdays, harness the expansive energies of Jupiter and Thor to manifest prosperity, abundance, and harmony in your life. Through mindful enchantments and offerings of gratitude, invite blessings to flow abundantly into your world.

Friday Magic

Love, Beauty, Romance, Healing, Trust, Protection, Loyalty, Womens Issues

Embrace the enchanting energies of Friday, dedicated to Venus, the goddess of love and beauty. This day is imbued with the magic of romance, fertility, and affection, revered by deities such as Eros, Aphrodite, and Freya. Here are some delightful enchantments to infuse your Friday with love and warmth:

Carry a rose quartz with you throughout the day to radiate gentle and loving vibrations, fostering harmony and compassion, even among difficult colleagues.

Work a tender Tarot spell to bless a friend's pregnancy with health and safety, invoking the nurturing energies of Venus to surround them with love and protection.

Engage in flower magic by enchanting a single pink rose for friendship and inner beauty, adorning your desk with its delicate presence.

Alternatively, empower a red rose for passion and desire, placing it in your bedroom to ignite the flames of romance.

Light rose-scented candles to evoke the essence of love and sensuality, inviting the tender touch of Eros to infuse your surroundings with passion and intimacy.

Share a romantic snack with your partner, indulging in ripe, red strawberries, known as love-inducing delicacies sacred to Venus and Freya. Let the sweetness of this fruit kindle the flames of affection and desire between you.

On Fridays, bask in the luminous glow of Venus's love and embrace the magic of romance, fertility, and connection. Through these enchantments, may you cultivate deeper bonds of love and intimacy, fostering warmth and harmony in your relationships.

Saturday Magic

Psychic, Illness, Death, Grounding, Transformation, and Spells

Embrace the potent energies of Saturday, ruled by Saturn, the god of karma and time. This day is steeped in protection, banishment, and the opportunity to tidy up any lingering magical clutter. Here are some enchanting rituals to elevate your Saturday:

Adorn yourself in black and deep purple. Embrace your inner drama and channel the witchy vibes of these hues, empowering your attire with layers of protection and strength.

Light black candles to absorb negativity and purple ones to enhance your magical wisdom and spiritual awareness, infusing your space with transformative energies.

Incorporate garden witchery into your spells by working with plants like the pansy (in black or purple), morning glory vines, or the majestic cypress tree, tapping into their protective and grounding properties.

Carry obsidian, hematite, or jet tumbled stones to fortify your personal protection and ward off negative vibrations. Add these crystals to candle spells on Saturday nights for an extra boost of spellcasting potency.

Engage in a thorough house cleaning and cleansing ritual, harnessing the energies of Saturn to remove obstacles and purify your living space, allowing positive energies to flow freely.

Conclude the bewitching week with a powerful invocation to Hecate, goddess of protection and guidance, seeking her blessings for strength and clarity in your endeavors.

On Saturdays, embrace the transformative powers of Saturn, cleansing your space, fortifying your protections, and preparing for new beginnings.

Magical Timing and Planets

In magical practice, it's essential to consider the influence of all the planets, not just the Moon. Tracking the positions of the planets and aligning their energies can greatly enhance the effectiveness of your spells. Here are some tips and considerations for incorporating planetary energies into your magical rituals:

Planetary Movement Tracking: Use resources available online to track the movements of the planets. Keep an eye on their positions relative to the Zodiac signs.

Intuitive Planning: Trust your intuition when planning the timing of your rituals. Consider which planetary energies align best with your intentions.

Sign Associations: Each Zodiac sign is ruled by a particular planet. When a planet transits through a sign, it amplifies the qualities associated with that sign. For instance, when Venus transits through Libra, it's an ideal time to focus on love and relationships.

Retrograde Planets: Planets occasionally appear to move backward in the sky, known as retrograde motion. Mercury retrograde, for example, is notorious for causing communication disruptions. Avoid initiating rituals related to communication during Mercury retrograde periods.

Record Keeping: Keep records of your spells and their outcomes. This will help you understand what works best for you and allow you to revisit and refine your magical practices over time.

By considering the movements and influences of the planets, you can enhance the effectiveness of your magical rituals and achieve your desired outcomes with greater precision.

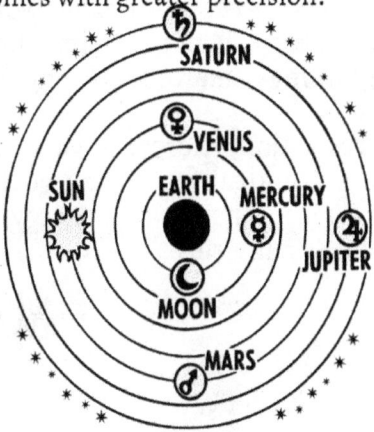

Magical Timing and Planets

Inner Planets

Understanding the inner planets is crucial for planning effective magical rituals. Here's a breakdown of each inner planet and how you can work with its energies:

The Sun: Despite being technically a luminary, the Sun is considered a planet in astrology. It represents vitality, self-expression, and personal power. Rituals planned when the Sun is in Aries, for example, can supercharge new beginnings and initiatives.

The Moon: The Moon is highly influential, governing emotions, intuition, and the subconscious mind. Focusing on the Sun and Moon positions can deepen your awareness of planetary energies and lay a foundation for more complex rituals.

Mercury: Mercury rules communication and intellect. During Mercury retrograde, communication tends to become disrupted. Therefore, avoid focusing on Mercury in your rituals during retrograde periods.

Venus: Venus symbolizes love, harmony, and balance. Work with Venus when it's direct to enhance your love life and cultivate positive energy. Venus passing through Aries can facilitate new beginnings and romantic opportunities.

Mars: Mars governs action, energy, and assertiveness. Rituals aligned with Mars are ideal for setting goals and initiating change. Mars in Aries intensifies this energy, especially when combined with the Sun in Aries.

Magical Timing and Planets

Outer Planets

For the outer planets, their slow movements and retrograde periods require a different approach:

Jupiter: Jupiter represents personal expansion and growth. Its slow movement through the zodiac requires awareness of its energy in the sign it transits. Retrograde periods are ideal for personal reflection and introspection.

Saturn: Saturn focuses on beliefs, values, and boundaries. Its slow orbit encourages introspection on how personal ideals align with the wider community, especially during retrograde periods.

Uranus: Uranus signifies creativity, intuition, and the unexpected. Its slow movement prompts reflection on one's role in a constantly changing world. Retrograde periods invite consideration of positive contributions to society.

Neptune: Neptune governs spirituality, intuition, and clairvoyance. Reflect on spiritual development and universal energy during its retrograde periods.

Pluto: Pluto represents transformation and evolution. Contemplate your impact on the earth and how to make positive contributions to the natural world during its retrograde periods.

By understanding and aligning with the energies of the inner and outer planets, you can create potent magical rituals that resonate with your intentions and goals.

Deities

Spellcrafting

Spellcrafting

A spell is a proactive way of manifesting your desires in life, tapping into your own purpose and energy using love and light.

As a witch, when you engage in spellcasting, you carry a significant responsibility. You wield creative power that can be used for the betterment of yourself and others, or for less noble purposes.

The pagan rede, a moral guideline, underscores the commitment to cause no harm and highlights the weight of being a witch. In our journey through life, we are constantly engaged in spellcrafting. Every word we utter holds power. Casting a spell brings this process into conscious awareness, allowing us to focus our energy and intentions toward our goals.

The Threefold Law is a fundamental principle in magic. It emphasizes the potent symbolism of the number three: the sending out of energy, its manifestation, and the return of karmic consequences. This law reminds us that whatever energy we project through spells will return to us threefold. It serves as a reminder to maintain high intentions, promoting positive experiences for ourselves and others. Positive magic yields the most beneficial outcomes, fostering a cycle of abundance and positivity.

Spellcrafting

What constitutes a spell varies widely, ranging from simple acts of intention-setting to elaborate rituals. Some spells can be completed swiftly, while others unfold over time, aligning with lunar cycles. These rituals often incorporate elements such as herbs, incense, candles, essential oils, and invocations, along with the blessing of deities.

Before delving into spellcasting, it's crucial to center and ground your energy through meditation and cleansing practices. Nurturing yourself is essential, as the aim of your spell is to bring positive change. Embrace rituals that connect you with the natural cycles of the sun and moon, fostering healing and empowerment. Cultivate confidence in your abilities and trust in your intentions.

Creating a protective circle prior to casting your spell is advisable. This can be achieved through visualization or by performing a ceremonial ritual, establishing a safe space for your magical work.

When crafting your spell, you have the option of using pre-written spells or tapping into your own creativity and intuition.

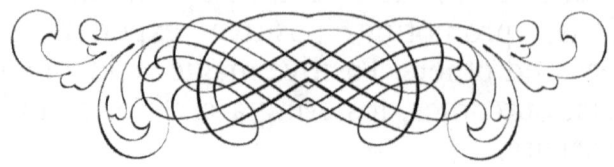

Spellcrafting Steps

1. Set Your Intention: Take a moment and clarify the purpose behind your spell. This clarity will help you communicate with deities or tap into your own magic and the universal energy. Focus on the positive outcomes you seek to manifest in your life and articulate your desires concisely.

2. Write Your Spell: While you can use existing spells, the most potent ones often originate from your own words and intentions. Express your desires authentically, drawing from your heart to establish a deep connection with universal energy.

3. Gather What You Need: Collect the tools and ingredients you'll use for your spell on your altar. Prepare in advance to ensure you have everything required when the time comes.

4. Cast Your Spell: Follow the steps outlined in your plan to cast your spell. Approach the process with confidence, firmly believing in the manifestation of your desires. You might choose to affirm with, "It is done," or "So it is," or "So mote it be," or perhaps something with a little pop culture, "I'm sexy, I'm cute, I'm popular to boot." Alternatively, you could incorporate a symbol representing your energy on your altar.

5. Record: Document your spell, including your intentions, ingredients, altar setup, spoken words, and emotional state. By keeping thorough records, it allows you to recreate the spell in the future. Additionally, consider revisiting your notes after a few months to reflect on the outcomes and your experiences.

Poetry As Spells

Writing poems as magic spells can offer several benefits, blending the creative process of poetry with the intention-setting and ritualistic aspects of spellwork. Here are some considerations:

Creative Expression: Poetry allows you to express yourself in unique and creative ways. Writing poems as magic spells provides an outlet for exploring emotions, desires, and intentions through metaphor, imagery, and symbolism.

Focus and Intention Setting: Crafting a poem requires concentration and clarity of thought. When writing a poem as a spell, you must carefully consider intentions and the words you choose to convey them. This process helps to clarify desires and focus energy towards specific goals.

Empowerment: Creating a poem imbued with magical intent can be an empowering experience. It allows you to take an active role in shaping your reality and influencing the world around you. By harnessing the power of language and creativity, you can feel a sense of agency and control over your life.

Connection to the Divine: Writing poems as magic spells can deepen your connection to the divine, whether that be through deity, nature, or universal energy. The act of crafting a spell can be a form of prayer or invocation, inviting divine guidance and assistance in manifesting desires.

Manifestation and Transformation: Just as traditional spells are believed to bring about change in the physical or spiritual realm, writing poems as magic spells can facilitate manifestation and transformation. The act of writing and reciting the poem can help to align your thoughts, emotions, and actions with your intentions, paving the way for desired outcomes.

Ritual and Ceremony: Incorporating poetry into magical rituals adds depth and symbolism to the practice. Reciting a carefully crafted poem can serve as a focal point for ritualistic activities, helping to create a sacred space and enhance the overall experience of the spellwork.

Personal Growth and Reflection: Writing poems as magic spells can be a deeply personal and introspective process. It encourages self-reflection, introspection, and exploration of your innermost desires and motivations. Through the act of writing, you may gain insight into yourself and aspirations, fostering personal growth and self-awareness.

Affirmation As Spells

Affirmations, likened to magic spells, bolster creativity and confidence in writing.

Affirmations counter negative beliefs, rewiring the brain alongside gratitude. Supported by decades of research, affirmations can replace harmful narratives with empowering ones.

Scientific studies have demonstrated affirmations' myriad of benefits, from enhancing creativity to reducing stress. MRI scans have show brain activation in reward centers and soothing of alarm processes in the brain.

To harness affirmations effectively:

Identify Your Intention: Determine what aspect of your life you want to change or improve. This could be related to your writing, personal growth, relationships, or any other area you wish to focus on.

Recall Past Successes: Reflect on past instances where you've achieved what you desire or overcame obstacles. Remember the feelings associated with these successes to ground your affirmations in reality.

Craft Positive Affirmations: Formulate positive statements in the present tense that reflect your intention. For example, instead of saying "I am not afraid of feedback," say "I confidently welcome and learn from feedback."

Make Them Personal and Specific: Tailor your affirmations to your unique situation and goals. Be specific about what you want to manifest in your life.

Repeat Regularly: Speak your affirmations aloud multiple times a day, ideally incorporating them into your daily routine. Repetition helps reinforce the message to your subconscious mind.

Believe and Visualize: As you repeat your affirmations, believe in their truth and visualize yourself already experiencing the outcomes you desire. This helps strengthen the power of the affirmations.

Use with Intent: Treat affirmations as intentional spells, focusing your energy and attention on manifesting your desires. Stay open to receiving the positive changes you're affirming.

Stay Consistent and Patient: Affirmations may take time to yield results, so be patient and consistent in your practice. Trust in the process and continue to affirm your intentions regularly.

Intention Setting in Spells

Intention in witchcraft is the act of clearly expressing your desires to the universe or your chosen spiritual entities. It forms the foundation of spells and rituals, directing your personal energy towards a specific outcome.

When crafting a spell, intention focuses your energy into a precise action or ritual, effectively communicating your needs or desires to the universe. Without intention, magic lacks direction and purpose.

Before setting your intention, it's crucial to define your desires with clarity and specificity. Avoid using phrases like "I want" or "I hope," as they may only manifest as wanting or hoping. Instead, phrase your intention as if it's already happening or happened, using "I" and "me" language as well as past tense.

Additionally, include a time constraint to specify the duration of your intention's manifestation. This ensures that your desires are fulfilled for as long as needed.

It's essential to keep your intentions realistic and achievable, especially for beginners. Simple and attainable goals are more likely to manifest successfully.

Reflecting on your motives and meditating to connect with your higher self can help you set meaningful and accurate intentions. Take time to understand your desires thoroughly before expressing them to the universe. Remember, it's normal to revise your intentions as you gain clarity and insight into your needs.

Spell Crafting Considerations

When crafting a spell, it's essential to consider various factors to enhance its effectiveness. Here's a breakdown of key elements to include when creating spell notes:

Date: Note the specific date of your spellwork, including the day of the week and the month.

Place: Identify the location where you'll perform the spell. This could be indoors or outdoors, depending on your preference and the nature of the spell.

Time: Record the time of day when you'll conduct the spell. Consider factors such as sunrise, sunset, or specific planetary hours for optimal energy alignment.

Season: Take note of the current season, as seasonal energies can influence the effectiveness of your spell. Consider whether it's fall, winter, spring, or summer.

Sabbat: If applicable, specify any relevant Sabbats or pagan holidays that coincide with your spellwork.

Moon Phases: Consider the phase of the moon, as it can affect the energy available for your spell. Note whether it's a new moon, full moon, waxing, or waning phase.

Zodiac: Check the current astrological sign of the moon or other relevant celestial bodies, as astrological influences may align with your spell's intention.

Element: Identify the primary element associated with your spell, such as earth, air, fire, or water. Aligning your spell with the corresponding element can enhance its potency.

Color Symbolism: Choose colors that resonate with your intention and correspond to your spell's purpose. Each color carries its own symbolic meanings and energetic properties.

Spell Crafting Considerations

Intention: Clearly define the intention of your spell, stating what you wish to manifest or achieve.

Deck (Tarot): If using tarot cards as part of your spellwork, specify the deck you'll use and any specific cards you'll draw.

Deity: If invoking deities or spirits, specify the names or aspects of the entities you'll call upon for assistance.

Herbs: List any herbs or botanicals you'll incorporate into your spell, along with their magical properties.

Crystals: Identify any crystals or gemstones you'll use, noting their metaphysical properties and significance to your spell.

Other Supplies: Include any additional tools or materials needed for your spell, such as candles, incense, oils, or ritual items.

Steps Taken: Document the specific actions and rituals performed during your spellwork, including any chants, invocations, or gestures.

Reflections & Thoughts: After completing the spell, reflect on your experience and any insights gained. Note any observations or feelings that arose during or after the spellwork.

By documenting these elements in your spell notes, you can create a comprehensive record of your magical practice and enhance your understanding of spellcraft over time.

Color Associations

Color plays a significant role in magic and ritual practices, as different colors are believed to carry distinct energies and qualities that can influence the outcome of spells and rituals. Here is a summary of common colors used in magic, along with their associated qualities and purposes:

Red:
Qualities: Passion, courage, strength, intense emotions.
Used in magic for: Love spells, physical energy, health, willpower.

Orange:
Qualities: Energy, attraction, vitality, stimulation.
Used in magic for: Adaptability to sudden changes, encouragement, empowerment.

Yellow:
Qualities: Intellect, inspiration, imagination, knowledge.
Used in magic for: Communication, confidence, divination, study.

Green:
Qualities: Abundance, growth, wealth, renewal, balance.
Used in magic for: Prosperity, employment, fertility, health, good luck.

Blue:
Qualities: Peace, truth, wisdom, protection, patience.
Used in magic for: Healing, psychic ability, harmony in the home, understanding.

Violet:
Qualities: Spirituality, wisdom, devotion, peace, idealism.
Used in magic for: Divination, enhancing nurturing qualities, balancing sensitivity.

White:
Qualities: Peace, innocence, illumination, purity.
Used in magic for: Cleansing, clarity, establishing order, spiritual growth, understanding.

Color Associations

Black:
Qualities: Dignity, force, stability, protection.
Used in magic for: Banishing and releasing negative energies, transformation, enlightenment.

Silver:
Qualities: Wisdom, psychic ability, intelligence, memory.
Used in magic for: Spiritual and psychic development, meditation, warding off negativity.

Gold:
Qualities: Inner strength, self-realization, understanding, intuition.
Used in magic for: Success, health, ambition, finances, good fortune, divination.

Brown:
Qualities: Endurance, solidity, grounding, strength.
Used in magic for: Balance, concentration, material gain, home, companion animals.

Grey:
Qualities: Stability, contemplation, neutrality, reserve.
Used in magic for: Complex decisions, binding negative influences, reaching compromise.

Indigo:
Qualities: Emotion, fluidity, insight, expressiveness.
Used in magic for: Meditation, clarity of purpose, spiritual healing, self-mastery.

Pink:
Qualities: Affection, friendship, companionship, spiritual healing.
Used in magic for: Romance, spiritual awakening, partnerships, children's magic.

Casting a Circle

Casting a Circle

Circle-casting is a significant practice in witchcraft, serving to create a sacred space outside of time where magick can be performed effectively. While not always necessary, it becomes pertinent in group rituals or when maximizing the efficacy of magickal workings.

The process of casting a circle can vary widely among traditions, ranging from simple to elaborate rituals. At its core, circle-casting establishes a liminal space where magickal potential is heightened, energy can be focused, and unwanted influences are kept out.

Aligning circle-casting with the principles of the Witches Pyramid involves calling upon the cardinal directions and their corresponding elements to fortify the circle during ritual.

Various ritual tools can be used to cast a circle, such as a wand, ritual dagger, or even one's finger. A common practice involves drawing the circle clockwise while invoking the energies of the elements.

Casting a Circle

Acknowledging specific entities associated with each direction, such as Watchers or Archangels, can further enhance the circle's protection and amplify the magickal workings.

It is crucial to dismantle the circle after completing ritual and spell work to prevent energy buildup and potential side effects. This can be done by undoing the circle in a counterclockwise direction, thanking any spirits or deities called upon, and bidding them farewell.

Circle-casting can be a foundational practice in witchcraft, creating a sacred space where practitioners can work magick safely and effectively. It is not a requirement for an individual practitioner or anyone at all. Do what feels right to you.

Calling the Quarters

I call upon the Spirts of the North: Guardians and beings of Earth. Please bless this circle with grounding and nurturing.

Hail and welcome!

I call upon the Spirts of the East: Guardians and beings of Air. Please bless this circle with intellect and imagination.

Hail and welcome!

I call upon the Spirts of the West: Guardians and beings of water. Please bless this circle with love and cleansing.

Hail and welcome!

I call upon the Spirts of the South: Guardians and beings of Fire. Please bless this circle with passion and strength.

Hail and welcome!

Casting Your Circle
Sweep the area of your circle with a broom or besom (symbolically if outside). Use a wand, hand, or sword to cast the circle. Walk clockwise three times. Visualize the sphere or dome of protection. Cleanse and strengthen with incense, saying, "I call upon the powers of fire and air to protect and consecrate this circle." Then, sprinkle a mixture of salt and water around your circle, saying, "I call upon the powers of earth and water to protect and consecrate my circle."

Including Deities and Spritis
After calling the corners, you may invite gods, goddesses, patrons, spirtes and others to join your circle.

Closing Your Circle
After your ritual is enabled, walk around your circle thrice in a counter-clockwise direction. Thank the elements and deities you invited to participate in your ritual. Direct the energies you worked with intent to the desired recipient.

Witch's Pyramid

To Know
Latin: Nascere
Element: Air
Direction: East
To know is the witch's knowledge and understanding of their craft.

To Dear
Latin: Audere
Element: Water
Direction: West
To Dare is the witch's courage to be different and face their fears.

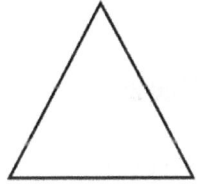

To Will
Latin: Velle
Element: Fire
Direction: South
To Will is the witch's conviction and passion for their beliefs and practices.

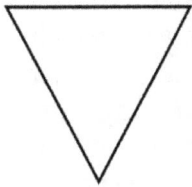

To Keep Silence
Latin: Tacere
Element: Earth
Direction: North
To Keep Silence is the witch's power of listening and keeping secret knowledge.

To Go
Latin: ire
Element: Spirit
Direction: Within
To Go is the witches ability to balance an evolve.

Spirit

Witch's Pyramid

The Witches Pyramid serves as a guiding principle for understanding what it means to be a witch, outlining the fundamental principles we adhere to and the cardinal directions along with their corresponding elements, which are essential during ritual.

To Know:
To Know embodies the element of air and corresponds to the east. It represents the mind and its role in witchcraft, including learning, visualization skills, and expanding consciousness to enhance psychic abilities. Being a witch involves being a lifelong learner, constantly seeking knowledge, and embracing the mysteries of the craft. Developing psychic abilities is essential for effective spellwork and manifestation.

To Dare:
To Dare corresponds to the west and the element of water. As the element of water symbolizes emotions, the unconscious mind, and initiation, To Dare involves being authentic in a world that may encourage conformity. It requires courage to pursue one's dreams and take risks, essential qualities for practicing magick and exploring the occult. To Dare also entails embracing experimentation and delving into the hidden aspects of the craft.

Witch's Pyramid

To Will:
To Will represents the cardinal direction of the South and the element of fire. It pertains to manifestation, energy, and the initial spark required for casting intentions. Fire symbolizes power, creation, and destruction, highlighting the potency and responsibility inherent in magick. Practitioners must harness their willpower and focus their intent to manifest their desires effectively.

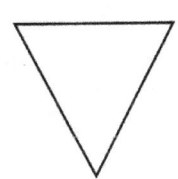

To Keep Silent:
To Keep Silent symbolizes the cardinal direction of the north and the element of earth. It emphasizes the importance of secrecy in magical workings to avoid interference from external influences and maintain the integrity of one's spells. Keeping one's craft hidden was historically essential for survival during periods of persecution, and it continues to serve as a means of protecting one's practice from scrutiny. Additionally, it serves as a caution against misuse of magick and underscores the need for discretion in sharing occult knowledge.

Witch's Pyramid

To Go:
To Go, introduced by Aleister Crowley, corresponds to the element of spirit and signifies the culmination of the witch's journey. It involves incorporating spiritual practices into daily life, walking the path of enlightenment, and serving others, oneself, and deity. By integrating spirit into their practice, witches tap into the anima of existence, bringing the other elements to life and deepening their connection to the divine.

Spirit

In essence, the Witches Pyramid provides a framework for witches to navigate their spiritual journey, emphasizing the importance of knowledge, courage, willpower, secrecy, and spiritual integration in their practice.

Performing a Ritual

1. Prepare Your Space
Start by clearing the energy in your space. You can do this by using a smudge stick, ringing a bell, or simply clapping your hands.

2. Cast The Circle
Create a protective barrier around yourself by casting a circle before each magical ritual. This circle becomes a sphere that envelops you and your magical workspace, providing a safe and impenetrable environment for your magic.

3. Invoke the Elements
Invoke the elements of Earth, Air, Wind, and Fire. Light a candle representing each element to enhance the power of your magic.

4. Call Upon Deity or Spirit
Call upon the presence of the goddess or god you have chosen for your practice. Alternatively, invoke spirit or universal energy, whatever resonates with you.

5. Conduct Your Ritual
Have a clear intention for your ritual and proceed through each step with focus and purpose.

6. Express Gratitude
Thank the deity and the elements for their presence and assistance. Then, release them with words of gratitude and extinguish the candles.

7. Close the Circle
At the conclusion of the ritual, release the energy and protection of the circle you have created. To close the circle, use your wand or athame to spin counterclockwise three times, dispersing the protective light. Thank the spirits and elements for their presence, signifying the closing of the circle.

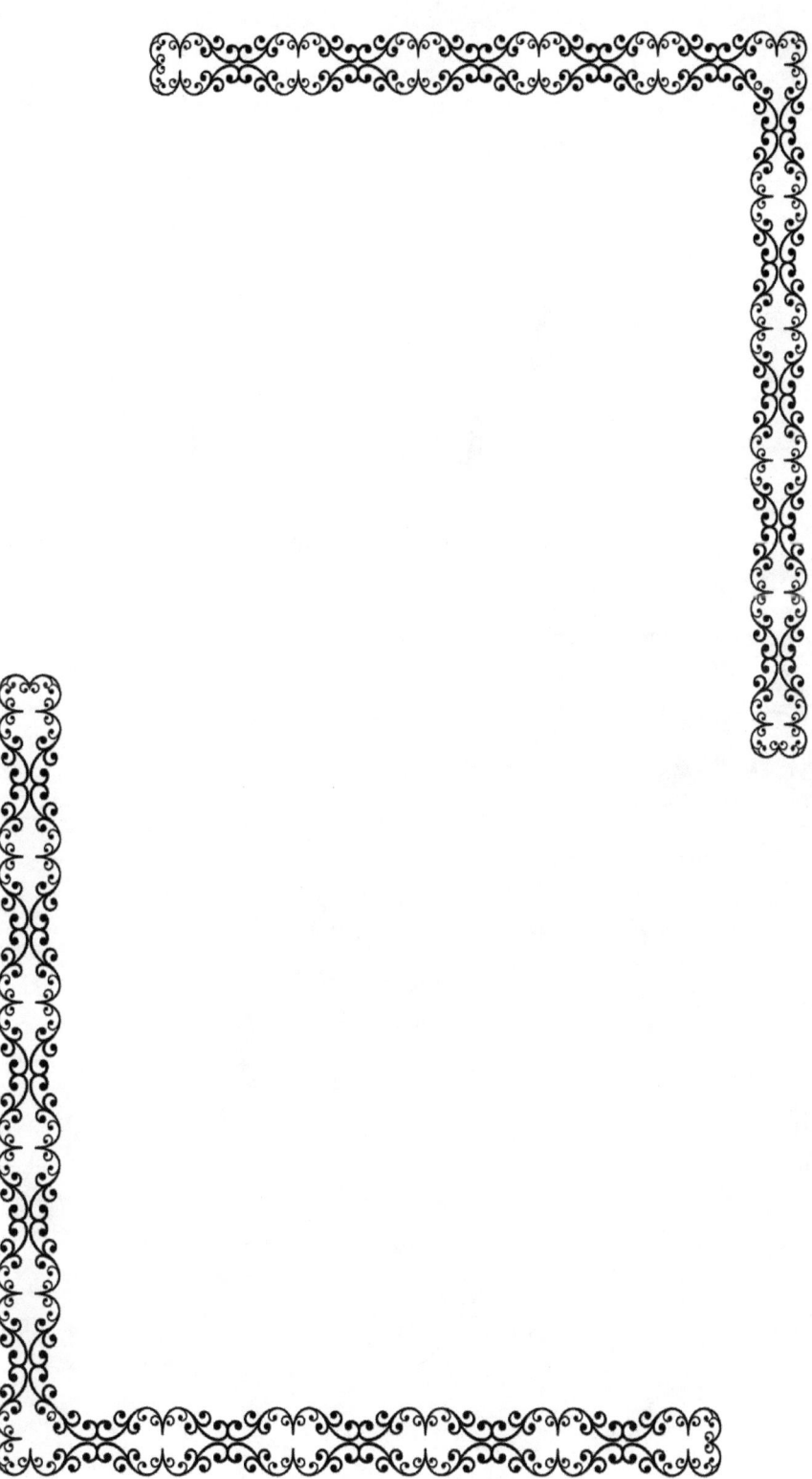

Divination

Abacomancy

Abacomancy, also referred to as Amathomancy, stands as a distinctive form of divination rooted in the analysis of patterns discerned within substances like dust, dirt, silt, sand, or even the ashes of the departed.

Etymology:
The term derives from the Greek word "amathos," signifying sand.

Methods:
Practitioners engage in the art of reading these patterns, believing they hold glimpses of the future. By scattering the particles onto a flat surface, whether it be soil, sand, or the remnants of ash, readers then meticulously observe for emerging shapes or symbols.

Various patterns may emerge, ranging from lines and triangles to spirals and hearts. For instance, an abundance of lines might foretell an imminent journey of significant length. The presence of a triangle signifies a balance of power across all its sides, while the appearance of a heart symbolizes matters of love and affection.

Aeromancy

Aeromancy, an ancient divinatory practice, encompasses the art of fortune-telling through the observation and interpretation of atmospheric phenomena. Whether it be the rumbling of thunder, the crackling of lightning, the patter of raindrops, or the gusting of wind, practitioners of aeromancy discern messages and omens from these natural occurrences.

Each atmospheric phenomenon carries its own symbolic significance, with thunder representing power and authority, lightning sudden insights or revelations, rain embodying cleansing or renewal, and wind signifying movement or change. By paying attention to these subtle shifts in weather patterns, practitioners can gain valuable insights into various aspects of life, from impending changes in fortune to guidance on important decisions.

Engaging in aeromancy allows individuals to forge a deeper connection with nature and tap into its inherent wisdom. It is a deeply personal and intuitive practice, relying solely on one's connection with the natural world and their ability to interpret its signals. Unlike some forms of divination that require specific tools or equipment, aeromancy demands only an attentive mind and a keen eye for the subtle rhythms of the elements.

Next time you're outside, take a moment to observe the weather and see what messages come through for you. Sometimes, it's a gut feeling or a sense of knowing that can't be explained—it's like nature speaking directly to you. Embrace the magic of being present in the moment and connecting with the natural world around you. Who knows what secrets the sky might be whispering to you?

Aeromancy

Remember, interpretations may vary, and mistakes can be made. It's all part of the learning process. So, take a deep breath, look up at the sky, and let the wisdom of the elements guide you on your journey.

Common interpretations in aeromancy include:

Thunder: Represents power, authority, and strength. It can indicate significant events or moments of realization.
Lightning: Symbolizes sudden insights, revelations, or flashes of inspiration. It can signify breakthroughs or moments of clarity.
Rain: Embodies cleansing, renewal, and emotional release. It can indicate a fresh start or the washing away of negativity.
Wind: Signifies movement, change, and transition. It can suggest opportunities for growth or the need to adapt to new circumstances.
Clouds: Reflect uncertainty, confusion, or hidden obstacles. The shape, color, and movement of clouds can provide additional insights into the situation.
Clear Skies: Symbolize clarity, peace, and harmony. It can indicate smooth sailing or a period of tranquility.
Fog: Represents confusion, uncertainty, or feeling lost. It may suggest the need to trust your instincts and proceed with caution.
Storms: Symbolize turbulence, challenges, or conflicts. They can indicate a period of upheaval or the need to weather a difficult situation.
Rainbows: Symbolize hope, promise, and new beginnings. They can signify a positive outcome or the fulfillment of wishes.
Sunset/Sunrise: Represents endings and beginnings. It can indicate the completion of a cycle or the start of a new phase in life.

Apacomancy

Apantomancy, an intriguing form of divination, delves into the interpretation of chance encounters with objects or animals, often seen as messages from the spiritual realm, the universe, or divine entities.

Rooted in the belief that everyday occurrences hold symbolic significance, apantomancy revolves around the interpretation of these chance encounters as meaningful omens or signs. Whether it's encountering an unexpected animal on your path or stumbling upon an unusual object, viewing these encounters as messages from the unseen forces guiding their lives is Apacomancy

While some symbols and interpretations have permeated mainstream consciousness, the meanings attributed to these chance encounters are largely personal and subjective. Each individual may interpret the symbols differently, drawing upon their own beliefs, experiences, and intuition to decipher their significance.

One of the notable aspects of apantomancy is its accessibility and simplicity. Unlike some forms of divination that require specialized tools or rituals, apantomancy requires nothing more than an open mind and a willingness to observe and interpret the signs encountered in daily life. By cultivating awareness of these chance encounters, practitioners can enhance their psychic development and deepen their connection to the spiritual realm.

Arithmancy

Arithmancy and Numerology both delve into the mystical significance of numbers, yet they approach the subject from slightly different angles. While Numerology assigns spiritual meaning to numbers, Arithmancy focuses on analyzing these numbers for insights and revelations.

In essence, Numerology serves as the broader umbrella term for divination practices involving numbers, encompassing both the assigning of spiritual significance and the interpretation of numerical patterns. On the other hand, Arithmancy specifically emphasizes the analytical aspect, delving into the deeper meanings and implications behind numerical sequences.

Although the terms Arithmancy and Numerology are often used interchangeably in common parlance, they retain distinct nuances in their technical definitions. Additionally, ancient systems such as Gematria or Isopsephy, originating from civilizations like the Assyrians, Babylonians, and Greeks, provide rich historical precedents for the study of number divination.

Despite their ancient origins, Arithmancy and Numerology remain relevant and accessible in modern times, with practitioners across the world continuing to explore their mysteries. Whether you're seeking spiritual guidance or insights into personal and universal truths, the study and practice of number divination offer a pathway to deeper understanding and self-discovery.

Astrology

Astrology stands as a revered form of divination, harnessing the celestial dance of planets and stars to unravel the mysteries of fate and personality. With origins tracing back to ancient civilizations such as the Mesopotamians, Mayans, Indians, and Chinese, astrology has permeated cultures across the globe for millennia.

At its core, astrology revolves around the intricate interplay of celestial bodies, offering insights into individual destinies and collective trends. By studying the positions and movements of planets and stars at the moment of one's birth, astrologers discern patterns and potentials that shape a person's life path.

Tomaster astrology, one must first acquaint themselves with the fundamental building blocks of the craft. Begin by delving into the meanings and symbolism associated with each planet, understanding their unique energies and influences. From there, immerse yourself in the rich tapestry of the zodiac signs, exploring their archetypal traits and characteristics.

Next, venture into the realm of astrological houses, which represent different areas of life and experiences. Each house holds its own significance, shedding light on various aspects of an individual's existence, from relationships and career to spirituality and personal growth.

As your knowledge deepens, you can delve into more advanced concepts within astrology, such as aspects, transits, and planetary alignments. These intricate configurations add layers of complexity to astrological interpretations, offering deeper insights into the dynamics at play in a person's chart.

Ultimately, mastering astrology is a lifelong journey of discovery.

Augury

Augury, an ancient practice steeped in mysticism, revolves around divining the future by observing the movements and behaviors of birds. Across diverse cultures and civilizations, birds have held a sacred significance, often being revered as messengers of the divine realm due to their ability to traverse the boundaries between heaven and earth.

Traditionally, augury encompasses various methods, offering insights into different aspects of the future. One approach involves observing birds in flight, where diviners interpret the birds' movements, interactions, and speed as omens foretelling future events.

Another method involves scrutinizing the actions of birds on the ground. Diviners would pose questions, scatter feed, and observe how the birds consume it. Over time, this practice evolved to include laying out feed in patterns resembling alphabets, with the diviner recording the letters pecked by the birds—a primitive precursor to the modern Ouija board.

Despite its historical significance, augury is not widely practiced by modern diviners, making it challenging to master for those drawn to its mystique. If one wishes to pursue augury today, they may need to delve into ancient texts for guidance or create their own personalized system of interpretation, adapting the ancient art to suit contemporary sensibilities.

Automatic Writing

Automatic Writing, involves harnessing the power of the subconscious mind to channel messages from various sources, including spirits, one's higher self, and otherworldly entities. The practice requires nothing more than a pen, paper, and a willingness to let go and allow the words to flow freely.

To begin, clear your mind of any distractions and open yourself to the possibility of receiving messages from beyond. With pen in hand and paper before you, enter a state of receptivity, allowing your subconscious to take the reins.

During the process of automatic writing, words, sentences, and even entire messages may pour forth onto the page without conscious effort. Some practitioners describe feeling as though they are merely a vessel through which the messages are channeled, while others experience a heightened sense of connection with their inner wisdom or spiritual guides.

The messages received through automatic writing can offer insights, guidance, and inspiration, covering a wide range of topics from personal growth and spiritual development to practical advice and future predictions. It's important to approach the practice with an open mind and a spirit of curiosity, allowing the messages to unfold naturally without judgment or preconceived notions.

Bibliomancy

Bibliomancy, a fascinating form of divination, taps into the wisdom and guidance found within the pages of books. Unlike some other divinatory practices, Bibliomancy is refreshingly straightforward—simply ask for guidance, open a book, and read the page or paragraph that catches your eye.

While traditional choices for Bibliomancy often include religious or spiritual texts, the beauty of this practice lies in its simplicity and versatility. Any book, from a cherished novel to a random volume from your bookshelf, can serve as a conduit for divinatory insights.

The process of Bibliomancy is deeply personal, with the chosen passage offering a message that resonates uniquely with the seeker. Whether seeking clarity, inspiration, or guidance on a specific question or concern, Bibliomancy provides a direct line to the wisdom contained within the written word.

As you embark on your journey with Bibliomancy, approach the practice with an open heart and mind, trusting that the universe will guide you to the words you most need to hear. Allow intuition to be your compass as you explore the pages of books, knowing that the messages you receive hold the keys to deeper understanding and insight.

Osteomancy

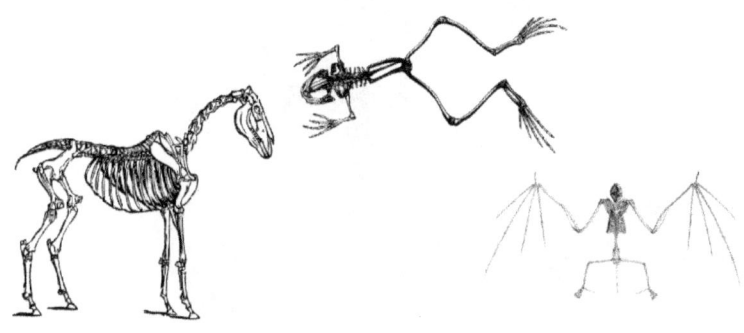

Osteomancy, commonly known as Bone Reading Divination, has experienced a remarkable resurgence in recent times.

This ancient form of divination, which incorporates the use of bones as tools, boasts a rich history spanning thousands of years and transcending continents and cultures. Practiced in regions ranging from Asia to Africa, the Americas, and beyond, bone casting holds profound significance within diverse spiritual traditions.

Central to bone reading is the symbolism imbued within each individual bone or piece used in the casting process. These symbolic meanings vary widely depending on the cultural background of the diviner and the specific traditions they adhere to, resulting in a diverse array of interpretations and practices.

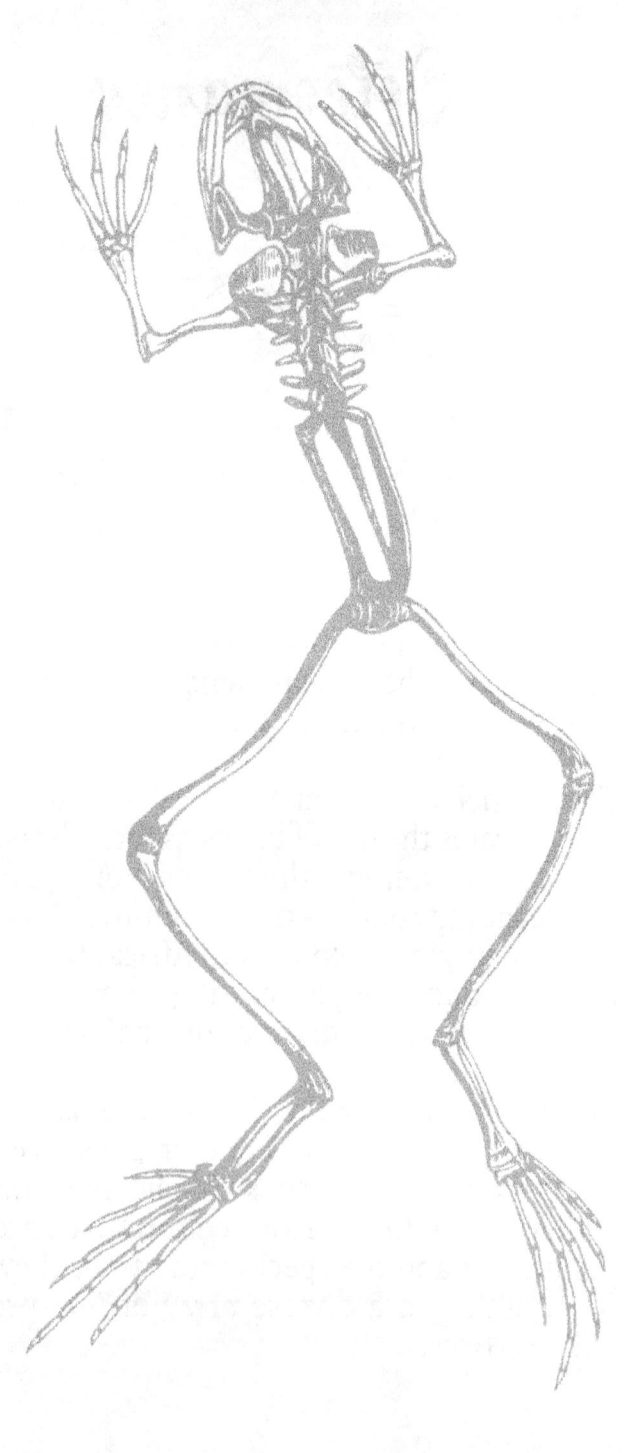

Capnomancy

Capnomancy, a form of fortune-telling, involves interpreting the shapes and patterns formed by smoke from various sources such as candles, fire, burning herbs, or incense. Similar to gazing at clouds to discern images and symbols, capnomancy invites practitioners to find meaning in the swirling tendrils and wisps of smoke.

For those adept at discerning shapes and forms in clouds, capnomancy offers a natural extension of this skill, providing a unique opportunity to tap into the mysteries of divination through the ethereal medium of smoke. Whether practicing alone or in a group setting, the process of capnomancy unfolds as practitioners observe the movements and configurations of smoke, allowing their intuition to guide them in deciphering the messages hidden within.

As with any form of divination, capnomancy requires patience, practice, and a willingness to trust one's instincts. By attuning to the subtle nuances of smoke patterns and embracing the intuitive insights they evoke, practitioners can unlock a realm of mystical wisdom and gain profound insights into the workings of fate and fortune.

Casting

Casting, akin to Osteomancy or Bone Reading, involves the act of tossing charms and interpreting their placement or arrangement in relation to each other. Unlike Osteomancy, which specifically utilizes bones for divination, Casting encompasses a broader range of materials and objects.

In Casting, practitioners throw an assortment of charms onto a divination board or surface, observing how they land and interact with each other. This method allows for intuitive interpretation of the patterns and configurations formed by the charms upon landing.

The charms used in Casting can vary widely, ranging from specially crafted sets like The Magpie Oracle to homemade collections assembled from keys, thimbles, nuts, seeds, or other found objects. Whether purchasing intricately designed gold charms or collecting items encountered during daily walks, the choice of charms is entirely personal and reflective of the practitioner's preferences and intuition.

With Casting, the diviner has the freedom to imbue each charm with symbolic meaning or significance, allowing for a deeply personalized approach to divination. As charms are tossed and arranged, the practitioner can glean insights and guidance from the patterns that emerge, unlocking the mysteries of fate and fortune in a manner that resonates uniquely with them.

Ceromancy

1. Begin by melting wax carefully, using a double boiler or bain-marie if necessary.

2. Once the wax has liquefied, gently pour it into a dish of ice-cold water. Upon contact with the water, the wax will harden, forming shapes.

3. Allow the wax to solidify completely before removing it from the water. Handling it too quickly may alter or destroy the initial shapes.

4. After solidification, remove the wax and interpret the shapes formed. Consider the number and appearance of the shapes, as they may hold significance.

5. Particularly meaningful shapes can be transformed into amulets, preserved, or carried for protection or guidance as needed.

Chirognomy

Chirognomy, a captivating branch of hand divination, delves into the intricate details of a person's personality through the examination of their hand shape, fingers, and other distinctive features.

In contrast to traditional palmistry, which primarily focuses on interpreting the lines and creases of the palm, Chirognomy adopts a holistic approach by placing greater emphasis on the overall structure and characteristics of the hands and fingers. As a result, practitioners of Chirognomy utilize a diverse array of physical attributes, such as the size, shape, and proportions of the hands, as well as the length and positioning of the fingers, to discern insights into an individual's nature and disposition.

In contemporary palmistry practices, Chirognomy has emerged as a prominent and accessible method for hand analysis, with many modern palm reading resources placing significant emphasis on this approach. Aspiring practitioners will find that mastering Chirognomy is relatively straightforward, as it offers a streamlined and intuitive framework for understanding the intricacies of human personality through the study of hand morphology.

Chirognomy can provide valuable insights into the complexities of human character and behavior. With its focus on hand shape and structure, Chirognomy offers a fascinating lens through which to explore the mysteries held within the palms of our hands.

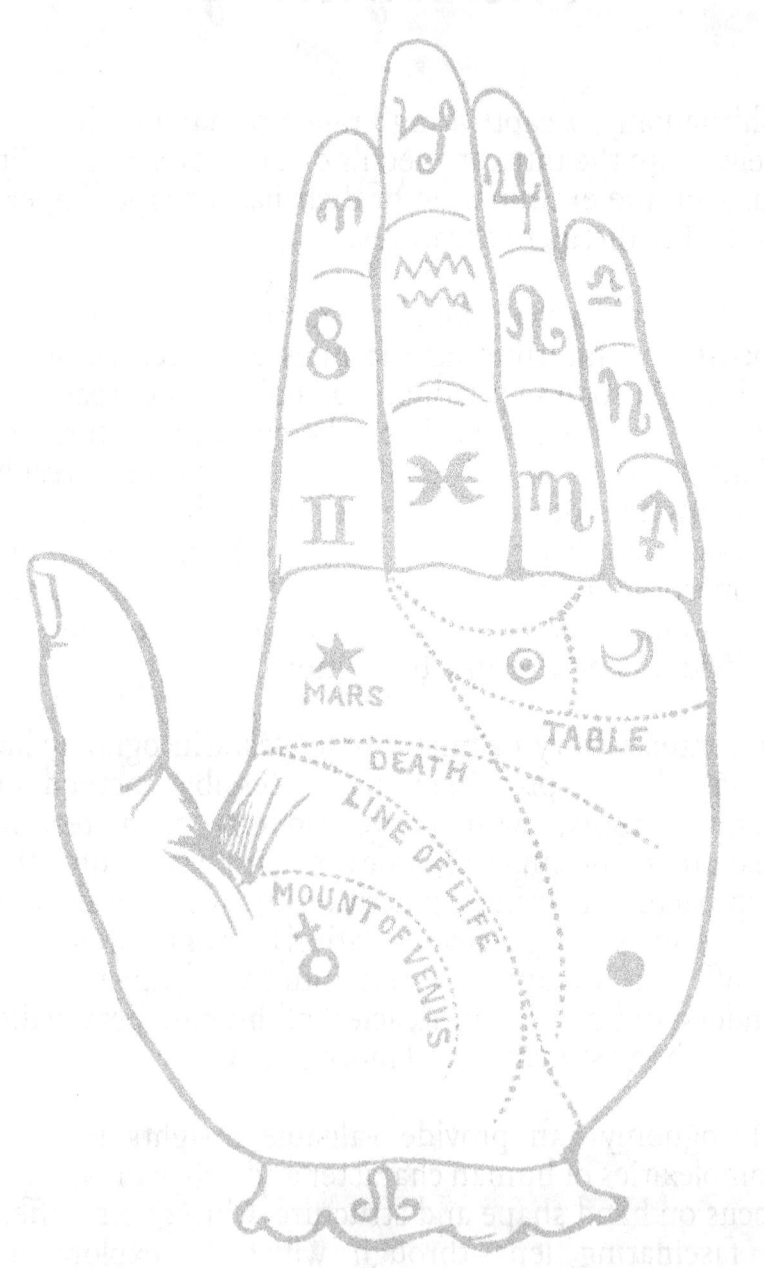

Cledonism

Cledonism is like hearing messages from the universe through everyday words or phrases—it's all about paying attention to the little signs and symbols that show up in your life and seeing them as messages from the universe.

Here's how it works:

Stay Open and Aware: The first step in practicing cledonism is to stay open and aware of your surroundings. Pay attention to the things people say, the signs you see, and the events that happen around you.

Notice the Signs: When something catches your attention—a word, a phrase, a song lyric, or even a random conversation—take a moment to notice it. It could be the universe trying to tell you something important.

Reflect and Interpret: Think about what the message might mean for you personally. Trust your intuition and go with whatever thoughts or feelings come to mind. Sometimes, the message might be crystal clear, while other times, it might require a bit of reflection to understand.

Cledonism

Act on the Message: Once you've interpreted the message, consider how you can apply it to your life. Is there a lesson to be learned? A decision to be made? Take action based on the guidance you've received.

Stay Curious: Cledonism is all about staying curious and open to the magic of the universe. Keep paying attention to the signs and symbols that show up in your life, and trust that the universe is always guiding you in the right direction.

Cledonism is a simple but powerful practice that can help you feel more connected to the world around you and more in tune with your own inner wisdom. So keep your eyes, ears, and heart open, and let the universe speak to you in its own unique way!

Conchomancy

Conchomancy is harnessing the mystical properties of seashells to unveil insights into the future. This practice encompasses various methods, including listening to the sound of waves within shells and employing them in casting divination.

One of the most common techniques in conchomancy involves placing a seashell against one's ear and attuning to the whispers of the ocean captured within. By interpreting the subtle nuances of these sounds, practitioners glean valuable guidance and prophetic messages.

Alternatively, conchomancy can be practiced through the art of casting divination, wherein shells are cast onto a surface and their positions analyzed for meaning. Each shell is imbued with significance based on its type, color, texture, and other attributes. Through careful interpretation, practitioners decipher the hidden wisdom conveyed by the arrangement of shells, akin to casting charms in other divinatory practices.

Conchomancy offers a simple yet profound method of seeking spiritual insight, as seashells are readily accessible and abundant in nature. Whether you are drawn to the soothing whispers of the sea or the tactile ritual of casting shells, conchomancy invites you to explore the mysteries of the ocean's depths and unlock the secrets of the future.

Crystal Ball Reading

Crystal ball reading, also known as scrying, is a method of divination steeped in mystique and ancient tradition. Utilizing crystal balls crafted from various materials such as quartz or glass, practitioners peer into these luminous spheres to unlock glimpses of the future.

To embark on a crystal ball reading, one must first clear the mind of distractions and allow the gaze to penetrate the depths of the crystal. As one gazes into the shimmering surface, images may begin to materialize, or intuitive insights may emerge from the depths of the subconscious.

While crystal ball reading holds a place of prominence in the realm of divination, mastering this art requires patience, dedication, and a finely tuned psychic acuity. Learning to interpret the symbols and visions revealed within the crystal ball demands diligent practice and a deep attunement to one's intuitive faculties.

Dice Divination

Dice divination is a method of divination that uses dice. You can use regular dice or special fortune-telling dice created for the purpose.

If you're using standard dice, it is customary to use two or three dice, not just one. Once you have your dice, all you have to do is ask your question, roll them, and then take note of the answer. If all dice contain an odd number, the answer is no. If all dice have revealed an even number, the answer is yes. If there is a mix between odd and even numbers, the answer is uncertain or unclear at this time.

Domino Divination

Domino divination is a method of fortune-telling, harnessing the symbolic power of regular domino tiles. In this divinatory practice, two domino tiles are drawn, and the numerical values on each are interpreted to unveil insights into the querent's fate.

Each combination of domino numbers carries its own unique significance, offering glimpses into various aspects of life and destiny. For instance, the presence of two blank tiles together may foretell looming misfortune, while the alignment of two sixes signifies a future brimming with happiness, success, and familial harmony.

This system of divination provides a straightforward yet profound means of tapping into the mysteries of fate and fortune.

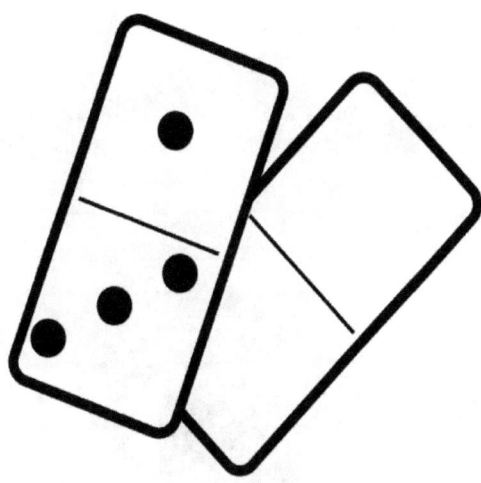

Dowsing

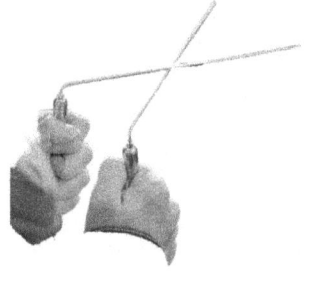

Dowsing encompasses two prominent methods of divination, each with its own distinct approach and purpose.

One method employs rods, commonly used to locate underground water sources or oil deposits, and even to uncover missing objects. The diviner holds the rods and allows them to guide them towards the sought-after target, relying on subtle movements or vibrations to indicate the presence of the desired element.

The other method of dowsing utilizes a pendulum made of crystal, glass, or metal. The diviner poses a question, holds the pendulum in their fingers, and observes its movements. The pendulum's sway is then interpreted, with different motions indicating yes, no, or maybe responses. This technique mirrors the interpretation of rings in Dactylomancy, offering insights into questions posed by the diviner.

Gypsy Fortune-Telling Cards

The history of Gypsy fortune-telling cards is intertwined with the broader tradition of Cartomancy, the practice of divination through the use of playing cards or other card-based systems. While the exact origins of Gypsy fortune-telling cards are difficult to trace definitively, their history is believed to stem from a blend of cultural influences, folklore, and mystical traditions.

Gypsy fortune-telling cards are thought to have emerged within Romani communities, also known as Gypsies, who are nomadic ethnic groups with roots in various regions of Europe, particularly Eastern Europe. The Romani people have a rich cultural heritage characterized by storytelling, music, and spiritual practices, including divination.

The cards themselves often feature imagery and symbols inspired by the Romani way of life, incorporating elements such as animals, nature, everyday objects, and traditional customs. Over time, these cards became associated with fortune-telling and were used by Romani fortune-tellers, or "gypsy" fortune-tellers, to provide insights into the past, present, and future.

The history of Gypsy fortune-telling cards is also influenced by the broader tradition of Cartomancy, which has ancient roots dating back to the use of playing cards for divination in medieval Europe. As playing cards spread across the continent, various methods of divination using cards developed, including Tarot cards and Lenormand cards, which are closely related to Gypsy fortune-telling cards.

In the 19th and early 20th centuries, interest in fortune-telling and divination surged across Europe, fueled by Romanticism, spiritualism, and a fascination with the mystical and occult. During this time, decks of Gypsy fortune-telling cards were produced commercially and marketed to a wider audience, popularizing the practice beyond Romani communities.

Today, Gypsy fortune-telling cards continue to be used by practitioners of divination and are appreciated for their accessibility, versatility, and rich symbolism. While their exact historical origins may be shrouded in mystery, these cards remain an enduring and cherished tool for those seeking guidance and insight into their lives.

The I Ching

The I Ching, also known as the Book of Changes, is an ancient Chinese divination text and philosophical classic that dates back thousands of years. It is one of the oldest and most revered divination systems in the world, with roots in Chinese cosmology, philosophy, and culture. The I Ching is based on the concept of change and the dynamic interplay of yin and yang energies.

Here's how the process of divination with the I Ching typically works:

Preparation: Before consulting the I Ching, the diviner usually takes a moment to center themselves and formulate a clear question or issue they seek guidance on. It's important to focus on a specific question or concern to receive a meaningful response.

Casting the Hexagrams: The I Ching consists of a series of 64 hexagrams, each composed of six lines, either broken (yin) or solid (yang). Traditionally, diviners cast the hexagrams using yarrow sticks, but modern methods include using coins or specialized dice. The diviner repeats a process of casting the sticks or coins six times to generate a hexagram.

Building the Hexagram: Based on the method used for casting (e.g., coin toss), the diviner assigns numerical values to the lines of the hexagram. For example, heads may represent a value of 3, and tails a value of 2. By adding up the values obtained from each cast, the diviner determines whether a line is solid (yang) or broken (yin).

Consulting the Oracle: Once the hexagram is generated, the diviner consults the corresponding text of the I Ching. Each hexagram is associated with a specific text passage that offers insights into the situation or question at hand. These passages are often poetic and symbolic, requiring interpretation based on the diviner's understanding of the context and the principles of the I Ching.

Reflection and Interpretation: After receiving the guidance from the I Ching, the diviner reflects on the hexagram and its associated text, considering how it applies to their question or situation. The diviner may also consider any changing lines within the hexagram, which indicate aspects of the situation that are in flux or undergoing transformation.

Application of Wisdom: Finally, the diviner applies the wisdom gleaned from the I Ching to their life or decision-making process. This may involve gaining clarity, understanding potential outcomes, or receiving advice on how to navigate challenges or opportunities.

The I Ching is valued not only for its divinatory insights but also for its profound philosophical teachings on the nature of change, balance, and harmony in the universe.

Kau Cim

Kau Cim, also known as "Chinese Fortune Sticks" or "Chi-Chi Sticks," is a form of divination practiced in East Asia, particularly in Chinese communities. The practice involves shaking a cylindrical container filled with numbered sticks until one stick emerges. Each stick is inscribed with a number that corresponds to a particular fortune or interpretation.

Here's how the process typically works:

1. The practitioner (or person seeking guidance) holds the container of sticks and concentrates on their question or situation.

2. They shake the container until a single stick falls out or is drawn out.

3. The number on the stick is then matched to a corresponding fortune or message found in a guidebook or scroll.

4. The interpretation of the fortune provides guidance or insight into the question or issue at hand.

Kau Cim is often practiced in temples or shrines dedicated to Chinese deities, particularly during festivals or special occasions. It is also used by individuals seeking guidance in various aspects of their lives, including relationships, health, finances, and career decisions.

The interpretation of the fortunes can vary depending on cultural and personal beliefs, as well as the specific guidebook or tradition being followed.

Kipper Cards

Kipper Cards are a type of oracle card deck used for divination and fortune-telling. Similar to Tarot cards, Kipper Cards feature symbolic images and illustrations that can be interpreted to gain insights into various aspects of life, including relationships, career, finances, and personal development. Here are some key points about Kipper Cards:

Origin: Kipper Cards originated in Germany during the late 19th century and became popular in the German-speaking regions of Europe. They were created by artist and fortune-teller Mrs. Susanne Kipper and her daughter.

Structure: A standard Kipper Card deck typically consists of 36 cards, each with its own unique image and meaning. The cards are numbered and usually contain a title or keyword that provides guidance for interpretation.

Themes: Kipper Cards often depict scenes from everyday life, such as people, objects, and situations commonly encountered in the context of relationships, work, and daily activities. The imagery focuses on practical and mundane aspects of life, making Kipper Cards particularly well-suited for providing concrete advice and insights.

Reading Method: Like other oracle card decks, Kipper Cards are used for readings by shuffling the deck and drawing cards randomly or in a specific spread. The reader then interprets the cards' meanings based on their symbolism, context within the spread, and any intuitive insights they receive.

Interpretation: Each Kipper Card has its own individual meaning, which can vary depending on the surrounding cards and the question or situation being addressed. Interpretations may involve considering the card's imagery, title, and numerical value, as well as intuitive impressions and personal associations.

Popular Spreads: There are several common spreads used with Kipper Cards, including the Grand Tableau, which involves laying out all 36 cards in a grid pattern to provide a comprehensive overview of past, present, and future influences in various areas of life.

Accuracy and Effectiveness: Many practitioners and enthusiasts find Kipper Cards to be accurate and insightful tools for gaining clarity and guidance on life's challenges and opportunities. The straightforward imagery and practical focus of Kipper Cards make them accessible to both beginners and experienced readers.

Kipper Cards

Lenormand Cards

Lenormand cards are a type of divination tool, similar to tarot cards, but with a distinct set of symbols and meanings. They are named after Marie Anne Lenormand, a famous French fortune-teller from the 18th century. Lenormand decks typically consist of 36 cards, each featuring a simple image or symbol that represents a specific concept or aspect of life.

These cards are often used for providing straightforward answers to questions or gaining insights into various situations. The Lenormand system relies heavily on the interpretation of card combinations and their proximity to each other within a spread, rather than individual card meanings alone.

While tarot cards may offer more nuanced and complex readings, Lenormand cards are prized for their clarity and directness. They can be particularly useful for practical, everyday questions and for gaining quick insights into specific areas of life such as love, career, or personal growth.

Using Lenormand cards involves shuffling the deck, drawing a certain number of cards, and laying them out in a specific pattern or spread. The reader then interprets the cards based on their positions and the combinations formed between them, offering guidance or advice based on the messages conveyed by the cards.

Overall, Lenormand cards are a powerful tool for divination, offering simple yet profound insights into life's mysteries and helping individuals navigate their paths with clarity and confidence.

Lenormand Cards

The Lenormand deck typically consists of 36 cards, each with its own distinct image and meaning. Here's a brief overview of the traditional meanings associated with each card:

Rider: News, messages, visitors, swift movement.
Clover: Luck, opportunity, chance, small joys.
Ship: Travel, journey, movement, progress.
House: Home, family, stability, security.
Tree: Health, growth, vitality, family history.
Clouds: Confusion, uncertainty, doubt, cloudy situations.
Snake: Deception, betrayal, temptation, complications.
Coffin: Endings, closure, transformation, loss.
Bouquet: Gifts, beauty, happiness, appreciation.
Scythe: Sudden change, risk, cutting ties, decisive action.
Whip: Conflict, argument, tension, repeated patterns.
Birds: Communication, conversations, gossip, socializing.
Child: New beginnings, innocence, simplicity, smallness.
Fox: Cunning, manipulation, deception, slyness.
Bear: Strength, authority, protection, maternal influence.
Stars: Hope, inspiration, guidance, dreams.
Stork: Change, transformation, new opportunities, birth.

Lenormand Cards

Dog: Loyalty, friendship, companionship, trust.
Tower: Institutions, isolation, authority, ambition.
Garden: Community, social gatherings, public events, networking.
Mountain: Obstacles, challenges, delays, isolation.
Crossroads: Choices, decisions, options, opportunities.
Mice: Loss, theft, worry, anxiety, erosion.
Heart: Love, romance, affection, relationships.
Ring: Commitment, contracts, promises, partnerships.
Book: Secrets, knowledge, learning, hidden information.
Letter: Communication, written messages, documents, news.
Man: Masculine energy, authority figure, significant male.
Woman: Feminine energy, authority figure, significant female.
Lily: Purity, peace, spirituality, maturity.
Sun: Success, happiness, warmth, enlightenment.
Moon: Intuition, emotions, cycles, subconscious.
Key: Solutions, opportunities, unlocking, answers.
Fish: Abundance, prosperity, wealth, opportunities.
Anchor: Stability, security, commitment, staying grounded.
Cross: Burdens, challenges, tests, sacrifices, destiny.

These meanings provide a foundation for interpretation, but it's essential to consider the context of the reading and the surrounding cards to gain a deeper understanding of the message being conveyed.

Lithomancy

Lithomancy, derived from the Greek words "lithos" meaning stone and "manteia" meaning divination, is a form of divination that involves interpreting the meanings of stones or crystals. While the term can encompass any type of rocks, in contemporary practice, it often refers to divination using polished or tumbled crystals, such as amethyst, quartz, or tiger's eye.

Each crystal in lithomancy is believed to possess its own unique energy and symbolism, which can be interpreted based on traditional associations, personal intuition, or metaphysical beliefs. For example, amethyst may be associated with spirituality and intuition, while rose quartz may symbolize love and emotional healing.

To practice lithomancy, one typically gathers a collection of crystals or stones, often selecting them based on their intuitive resonance or specific meanings. These stones are then placed in a container, such as a bag or a bowl, and mixed or shaken while focusing on a question or issue. After the stones have been shuffled, the diviner selects one or more stones from the container, either by reaching in blindly or by laying them out and choosing intuitively.

The stone or stones drawn are then interpreted based on their individual properties, energies, and symbolic meanings, as well as their relevance to the question or situation at hand. The diviner may consider factors such as color, shape, texture, and any intuitive impressions or associations that arise during the reading.

Lithomancy readings can offer insights, guidance, and potential outcomes related to a wide range of topics, including relationships, career, health, and personal growth. Like other forms of divination, the effectiveness of lithomancy often depends on the diviner's intuition, connection to the stones, and ability to interpret their messages accurately.

Ogham

Ogham is an ancient Celtic alphabet used primarily for inscriptions on stone monuments and other objects. It originated in Ireland and was later adopted by other Celtic regions, including Scotland and Wales. The Ogham alphabet consists of a series of strokes or notches carved into a central stemline or the edge of a stone, wood, or other material.

Each character in the Ogham alphabet represents a different sound, and the letters are grouped into four main categories known as aicmí, each associated with a different set of trees. These tree associations have led to the use of Ogham as a form of divination, known as Ogham divination or Ogham staves.

In Ogham divination, each letter of the Ogham alphabet is associated with specific trees, plants, or natural elements, as well as symbolic meanings and interpretations. Diviners may use sets of Ogham staves, wooden sticks or rods inscribed with Ogham characters, to perform readings similar to other forms of rune casting or oracle divination.

During a divination session, the diviner typically focuses on a question or issue and then draws a set number of Ogham staves from a bag or container. The arrangement and orientation of the staves are then interpreted based on their symbolic meanings, associations with trees or natural elements, and the diviner's intuitive impressions.

Ogham divination readings can provide insights, guidance, and perspectives on various aspects of life, including relationships, career, health, and spiritual growth. Like other forms of divination, the accuracy and effectiveness of Ogham readings depend on the diviner's skill, intuition, and ability to interpret the symbols and messages conveyed by the Ogham characters.

Oracle Cards

Oracle cards are a tool used for divination and spiritual guidance. Unlike traditional tarot cards, which follow a specific structure with 78 cards divided into major and minor arcana, oracle cards come in a wide variety of decks with different themes, imagery, and numbers of cards. They are often used for intuitive readings, personal reflection, and seeking guidance on specific questions or situations.

Oracle cards can feature diverse themes such as angels, animals, nature, mythology, chakras, affirmations, and more. Each deck typically comes with a guidebook that provides interpretations and suggested spreads, although users are encouraged to trust their intuition and interpret the cards in a way that resonates with them personally.

To perform a reading with oracle cards, the user typically shuffles the deck while focusing on their question or intention. They then draw one or more cards from the deck and interpret the imagery, symbols, and messages depicted on the cards. Some readers may also incorporate additional practices such as meditation, visualization, or journaling to deepen their connection with the cards and their intuitive insights.

Oracle cards are valued for their accessibility, versatility, and ability to provide gentle and supportive guidance. They can be used by individuals of all levels of experience, from beginners to seasoned practitioners, and are often used for daily affirmations, spiritual growth, and self-discovery. Whether used alone or in combination with other divination tools, oracle cards offer a flexible and empowering means of seeking insight, clarity, and inspiration in various areas of life.

Ouija Board

Ouija, also known as a spirit board or talking board, is a tool used for communicating with spirits or entities from the spirit world. It typically consists of a flat board marked with the letters of the alphabet, numbers 0-9, and other symbols such as "yes," "no," and "goodbye." Participants place their fingers lightly on a movable indicator called a planchette, and through a process of asking questions aloud, spirits are believed to guide the planchette to spell out answers or messages.

The origins of the Ouija board are somewhat unclear, but it gained popularity in the late 19th century as a parlor game and tool for spiritual communication. Its name is a combination of the French and German words for "yes" (oui and ja, respectively), reflecting its use of language-based responses.

Using a Ouija board typically involves one or more participants sitting around the board with their fingertips on the planchette. They may begin by asking a question aloud, such as "Is anyone there?" or "Can you communicate with us?" Then, they wait for the planchette to move on its own, guided by unseen forces. The planchette may glide across the board to select letters or spell out words in response to the questions asked.

Beliefs about the nature of the communication facilitated by Ouija boards vary widely.

Ouija boards have been a subject of controversy and debate, with some people warning of potential dangers associated with their use, such as opening portals to negative energies or attracting malevolent spirits. As a result, individuals are often advised to approach Ouija boards with caution and respect, to use them in a controlled and responsible manner, and to discontinue use if they experience feelings of fear or discomfort.

Palmistry

Palmistry, also known as chiromancy or palm reading, is the practice of interpreting the lines, shapes, and markings on the palm of a person's hand to reveal insights about their character, personality, strengths, weaknesses, and potential future events. It is an ancient form of divination that has been practiced for centuries in various cultures around the world.

The basic principle of palmistry is that the palm of the hand contains information about a person's life and character, and that by examining the lines, mounts, and other features of the palm, a skilled palm reader can uncover hidden truths and provide guidance.

Key elements of palmistry include:

Lines: The lines on the palm, such as the heart line, head line, and life line, are considered to represent different aspects of a person's life, emotions, intellect, and vitality. The length, depth, and curvature of these lines, as well as any breaks, forks, or other markings, are interpreted to reveal specific characteristics or events.

Mounts: The mounts are the fleshy areas of the palm beneath each finger. Each mount is associated with a particular planet and is said to represent different qualities or traits, such as creativity, ambition, or intuition. The size, shape, and texture of the mounts are examined to gain insights into a person's personality.

Fingers: The length, shape, and flexibility of the fingers are also considered in palmistry. Each finger is associated with a different element (earth, water, fire, air) and is said to correspond to different aspects of a person's nature, such as practicality, emotionality, passion, or intellect.

Other features: In addition to lines, mounts, and fingers, palmists may also consider other features of the hand, such as the shape of the nails, the texture of the skin, and any unusual markings or symbols.

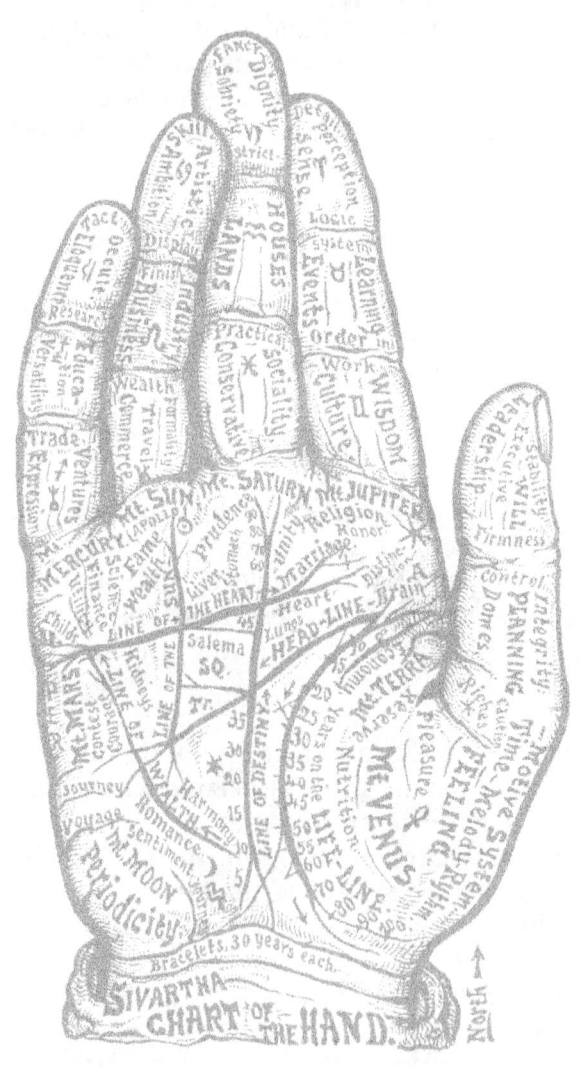

Playing Cards

Playing cards have been used for divination for centuries, with various systems and methods developed over time. One of the most popular systems is Cartomancy, which involves interpreting the meanings of the cards to gain insights into past, present, and future events, as well as into a person's character, relationships, and potential outcomes.

Here's a basic overview of how playing cards can be used for divination:

Deck: A standard deck of playing cards consists of 52 cards, divided into four suits: hearts, diamonds, clubs, and spades. Each suit contains thirteen cards, including numbered cards (2 through 10) and face cards (jack, queen, king), with each face card representing different personality traits or archetypes.

Shuffling: The first step in a card reading is to shuffle the deck thoroughly to mix up the cards and clear any previous energies. The querent (the person seeking the reading) may also be asked to shuffle the cards to infuse their own energy into the deck.

Drawing Cards: After shuffling, the reader draws a certain number of cards from the deck, typically based on the spread or layout being used for the reading.

Interpretation: Once the cards have been drawn and laid out, the reader interprets their meanings based on traditional associations, intuitive insights, and the positions of the cards within the spread.

Context: In addition to individual card meanings, the reader considers the overall context of the reading, including the querent's question or intention, the surrounding cards in the spread, and any patterns or themes that emerge during the reading.

Reflection and Guidance: The purpose of the reading is to provide insight, guidance, and clarity to the querent.

Playing card readings can cover a wide range of topics, including love, career, finances, health, and spirituality. While some readers prefer to use traditional interpretations and spreads, others may develop their own unique methods and approaches based on personal experience and intuition.

Playing Cards

Hearts:
Ace of Hearts: Love, new beginnings, emotional fulfillment
King of Hearts: Authority, emotional stability, generosity
Queen of Hearts: Compassion, nurturing, intuition
Jack of Hearts: Romantic interest, charm, emotional energy
10 of Hearts: Emotional fulfillment, joy, abundance
9 of Hearts: Dreams coming true, emotional well-being, satisfaction
8 of Hearts: Wish fulfillment, contentment, harmony
7 of Hearts: Inner guidance, decisions, choices
6 of Hearts: Memories, nostalgia, sentimentalism
5 of Hearts: Emotional ups and downs, changes, transitions
4 of Hearts: Emotional security, stability, home life
3 of Hearts: Happiness, celebration, social gatherings
2 of Hearts: Partnership, union, harmony

Diamonds:
Ace of Diamonds: Wealth, material abundance, new opportunities
King of Diamonds: Financial success, leadership, business acumen
Queen of Diamonds: Practicality, resourcefulness, financial security
Jack of Diamonds: Ambition, entrepreneurship, determination
10 of Diamonds: Abundance, prosperity, wealth
9 of Diamonds: Attainment, accomplishment, fruition
8 of Diamonds: Recognition, success, achievement
7 of Diamonds: Planning, assessment, evaluation
6 of Diamonds: Financial opportunities, material gains
5 of Diamonds: Adjustments, challenges, change
4 of Diamonds: Foundations, stability, security
3 of Diamonds: Practical skills, work, effort
2 of Diamonds: Financial decisions, balance, partnership

Playing Cards

Clubs:
Ace of Clubs: Success, achievement, new beginnings
King of Clubs: Authority, leadership, mastery
Queen of Clubs: Independence, creativity, ambition
Jack of Clubs: Energy, enthusiasm, action
10 of Clubs: Fulfillment, culmination, completion
9 of Clubs: Persistence, resilience, determination
8 of Clubs: Momentum, progress, movement
7 of Clubs: Perseverance, tests, challenges
6 of Clubs: Overcoming obstacles, success, victory
5 of Clubs: Adversity, struggle, competition
4 of Clubs: Structure, organization, stability
3 of Clubs: Expansion, growth, progress
2 of Clubs: Partnership, teamwork, cooperation

Spades:
Ace of Spades: Endings, transformation, challenges
King of Spades: Authority, intellect, wisdom
Queen of Spades: Introspection, self-discipline, resilience
Jack of Spades: Challenges, setbacks, adversity
10 of Spades: Transformation, completion, endings
9 of Spades: Fear, worry, anxiety
8 of Spades: Delays, restrictions, obstacles
7 of Spades: Hidden truths, illusion, deception
6 of Spades: Moving forward, change, transition
5 of Spades: Adversity, struggle, challenge
4 of Spades: Retreat, rest, recuperation
3 of Spades: Sorrow, heartbreak, loss
2 of Spades: Decisions, tension, conflict

Playing Cards

Pyromancy

Pyromancy is a form of divination that involves interpreting flames, smoke, or the patterns formed by fire. This ancient practice is rooted in the belief that fire possesses mystical properties and can reveal insights about the future or provide guidance.

There are several methods of pyromancy:

1. Flame Interpretation: Observing the behavior, movement, and intensity of flames from a candle, bonfire, or any other source of fire. Different flame shapes, colors, and movements are believed to convey different messages or omens.

2. Smoke Reading: Analyzing the patterns and movements of smoke rising from a fire. The direction, thickness, and shape of the smoke can be interpreted to gain insights into various situations or questions.

3. Scrying in Flames: Gazing into the flames of a fire or focusing on a specific area within the fire to induce a trance-like state and receive visions, symbols, or messages. Practitioners may see images or symbols that provide guidance or answers to their inquiries.

Candle Divination: Using candles as a focal point for divination by observing the way they burn, the shape of the wax drippings, or any unusual occurrences during the burning process. Each aspect of the candle's behavior is believed to carry significance.

Bonfire Rituals: Performing rituals or ceremonies around a bonfire and interpreting the flames as part of the ritual process. The size, brightness, and intensity of the fire are often considered important factors in these rituals.

Pyromancy requires concentration, intuition, and the ability to interpret subtle signs and symbols in the flames or smoke. Practitioners may also incorporate other forms of divination or ritual practices alongside pyromancy to enhance its effectiveness or gain deeper insights.

It's important to approach pyromancy with caution and respect for fire safety measures, as working with fire carries inherent risks.

Runes

Runes are ancient symbols used for divination, magic, and communication in various Germanic languages and cultures. The runic alphabet, known as the Futhark, consists of characters called runes, each with its own specific meaning and significance. Originally, runes were inscribed on stone, wood, or metal objects, but today they are often used on cards or as part of ritual practices.

The word "rune" itself means "mystery" or "secret" in Old Norse, reflecting the esoteric nature of these symbols. The runic alphabet is divided into several different sets, with the Elder Futhark being the oldest and most widely known. It consists of 24 characters, each representing a specific sound or concept.

The runes are not just letters but are also considered to be magical and symbolic entities with their own inherent power. They can be used for various purposes, including divination, protection, healing, and communication with spiritual forces. When used for divination, runes are typically cast onto a cloth or a surface, and the pattern in which they fall is interpreted to gain insights into the past, present, or future.

Interpreting runes requires intuition, knowledge of the runic meanings, and an understanding of the context in which they are being used. Each rune carries multiple layers of symbolism and can have different interpretations depending on its position, the surrounding runes, and the specific question or situation being addressed.

The meanings of runes can vary slightly between different runic traditions and practitioners, so it's essential to develop a personal connection with the symbols and trust your intuition when interpreting them.

Runes

Elder Futhark
Fehu (ᚠ): Wealth, abundance, prosperity.
Uruz (ᚢ): Strength, vitality, primal energy.
Thurisaz (ᚦ): Protection, defense, overcoming obstacles.
Ansuz (ᚨ): Communication, divine inspiration, wisdom.
Raido (ᚱ): Journey, travel, progress.
Kenaz (ᚲ): Creativity, illumination, transformation.
Gebo (ᚷ): Partnership, harmony, gifts.
Wunjo (ᚹ): Joy, happiness, fulfillment.
Hagalaz (ᚺ): Disruption, chaos, sudden change.
Nauthiz (ᚾ): Constraint, necessity, resistance.
Isa (ᛁ): Stillness, stagnation, challenge.
Jera (ᛃ): Harvest, cycles, patience.
Eihwaz (ᛇ): Endurance, perseverance, transformation.
Perthro (ᛈ): Mystery, chance, fate.
Algiz (ᛉ): Protection, defense, intuition.
Sowilo (ᛊ): Success, victory, enlightenment.
Tiwaz (ᛏ): Justice, leadership, self-sacrifice.
Berkano (ᛒ): Growth, fertility, renewal.
Ehwaz (ᛖ): Partnership, teamwork, movement.
Mannaz (ᛗ): Humanity, social connections, awareness.
Laguz (ᛚ): Intuition, unconscious, flow.
Ingwaz (ᛜ): Fertility, potential, internal growth.
Dagaz (ᛞ): Enlightenment, breakthrough, transformation.
Othala (ᛟ): Ancestral inheritance, home, roots.

Tarot

Tarot is a form of divination that uses a deck of cards to gain insight into past, present, and future events, as well as to explore personal spirituality and psychology. A typical tarot deck contains 78 cards, divided into two main categories: the Major Arcana and the Minor Arcana.

Major Arcana: These cards represent significant life themes, spiritual lessons, and archetypal energies. There are 22 Major Arcana cards, each with its own unique symbolism and meaning. Some of the most well-known Major Arcana cards include The Fool, The Magician, The High Priestess, The Empress, The Emperor, The Lovers, The Chariot, Strength, The Hermit, Wheel of Fortune, Justice, The Hanged Man, Death, Temperance, The Devil, The Tower, The Star, The Moon, The Sun, Judgement, and The World.

Minor Arcana: The Minor Arcana consists of 56 cards divided into four suits: Wands (or Rods), Cups, Swords, and Pentacles (or Coins). Each suit represents different aspects of life, such as creativity (Wands), emotions (Cups), intellect (Swords), and material aspects (Pentacles). Each suit contains ten numbered cards (Ace through Ten) and four court cards: Page, Knight, Queen, and King.

Tarot readings involve shuffling the cards while focusing on a question or situation, then drawing a specific number of cards and interpreting their symbolism and placement in relation to the question or issue at hand. Readers may use various spreads, such as the Celtic Cross, Three-Card Spread, or the One-Card Draw, to provide insight into different aspects of the querent's life or to address specific questions.

Interpretation of tarot cards can vary based on the reader's intuition, knowledge of symbolism, and personal associations with the cards. While some readers adhere strictly to traditional interpretations, others may incorporate their own insights and experiences into their readings.

Tasseomancy aka Tea Leaf Reading

Tasseomancy, also known as tea leaf reading or tasseography, is a form of divination that interprets patterns formed by tea leaves or coffee grounds left in a cup after the beverage has been consumed. This ancient practice dates back centuries and has roots in various cultures around the world, including China, the Middle East, and Europe.

Here's how tasseomancy typically works:

Preparation: To begin a tea leaf reading session, loose tea leaves are traditionally used, although some practitioners also use coffee grounds. The tea is brewed in a pot or cup without a strainer, allowing the leaves to remain in the liquid.

Pouring the Tea: The brewed tea is then poured into a cup, usually a white or light-colored cup with a wide rim. The person seeking the reading is encouraged to focus on a question or area of their life they would like guidance on while drinking the tea.

Leaving Residue: After drinking the tea, a small amount of liquid is left at the bottom of the cup, along with the tea leaves or coffee grounds. The cup is then swirled or inverted to allow the residue to coat the sides of the cup, creating patterns.

Interpretation: The reader examines the patterns formed by the leaves or grounds and interprets them based on their shape, size, position, and proximity to one another. The shapes may resemble various symbols, objects, or letters, each of which carries symbolic meaning.

Symbolism and Meaning: The interpretation of the symbols is highly subjective and can vary based on the reader's intuition, cultural background, and personal associations.

Context and Surroundings: The reader may also consider the overall context of the reading, including the querent's question or intention, as well as any other symbols or images that may be present in the cup.

Providing Guidance: The goal of tasseomancy is to provide insight, guidance, and reflection to the querent. The reader may offer interpretations and advice based on the symbols observed in the cup, helping the querent gain clarity and understanding about their current situation or future prospects.

Tasseomancy aka Tea Leaf Reading

Common Symbols

Animals: Animals appearing in tea leaves may represent various qualities or aspects of life. For example, a bird could symbolize freedom, messages, or opportunities, while a cat might signify intuition, independence, or mystery.

Shapes and Objects: Tea leaves may form shapes resembling everyday objects, such as keys, hearts, circles, or stars. These shapes can symbolize different themes or experiences. For instance, a key may suggest unlocking new opportunities or insights, while a heart could indicate love, affection, or emotional connections.

Plants and Flowers: Images of plants, trees, or flowers in tea leaves can carry symbolic meanings related to growth, renewal, and natural cycles. Different flowers may convey specific messages; for example, a rose could represent love, passion, or romance, while a sunflower might symbolize vitality, happiness, or success.

Symbols of Luck or Fortune: Some tea leaf symbols are associated with luck, fortune, or positive outcomes. These may include images of horseshoes, four-leaf clovers, or coins, which can suggest opportunities for prosperity, abundance, or good fortune ahead.

Letters, Numbers, or Symbols: Occasionally, tea leaves may form shapes resembling letters, numbers, or other symbols. These symbols could be interpreted as messages, guidance, or insights related to specific words, dates, or concepts. For example, seeing the letter "S" might represent a person's name or indicate a significant place or event starting with that letter.

Lines and Patterns: The arrangement of tea leaves and the patterns they form within the cup can also convey meanings. Lines, swirls, or clusters may suggest pathways, transitions, or areas of focus in the querent's life. For instance, a spiral shape might represent a journey of self-discovery or personal growth.

Emotions and States of Mind: Tea leaf symbols may reflect the querent's emotions, thoughts, or subconscious desires. Dark, dense leaves could indicate feelings of uncertainty or challenges, while light, airy patterns might suggest optimism, clarity, or new beginnings.

It's important to note that interpretations of tea leaf symbols can be highly subjective and may vary based on the intuition and experience of the reader, as well as the cultural context and personal symbolism of the querent.

Xylomancy

Xylomancy is a form of divination that involves interpreting messages or omens from wood or tree branches. The practice of xylomancy can vary depending on cultural traditions and individual beliefs, but it often involves observing the shape, texture, grain, and other characteristics of the wood or branches to discern insights about the future or receive guidance.

Here's how xylomancy is typically practiced:

Selection of Wood or Branches: The practitioner may gather wood or branches from specific types of trees, each of which may have its own symbolic associations or properties. Different woods are believed to carry distinct energies or vibrations that can influence the divinatory process.

Preparation and Focus: Before beginning the xylomancy session, the practitioner may take time to center themselves and focus their intention on receiving guidance or insights from the wood. This may involve meditation, prayer, or other rituals to attune to the energies of nature and the spirits associated with the trees.

Casting or Scrying: The practitioner may arrange the wood or branches in a particular pattern, such as scattering them on the ground or arranging them on a surface. They may then observe the shapes, patterns, and formations that emerge, paying attention to any symbols, images, or impressions that catch their attention.

Interpretation: Using intuition, symbolism, and personal insights, the practitioner interprets the messages or omens perceived within the wood or branches. This interpretation may involve identifying specific shapes, patterns, or images and associating them with meanings relevant to the querent's question or situation.

Reflection and Application: After completing the xylomancy session, the practitioner reflects on the insights received and considers how they may apply to the querent's life or circumstances. The messages gleaned from the wood or branches may offer guidance, validation, or new perspectives to consider moving forward.

As with any form of divination, xylomancy is best approached with an open mind, a spirit of reverence for nature, and a willingness to explore the mysteries of the natural world.

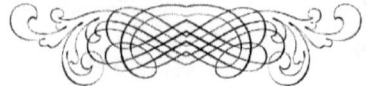

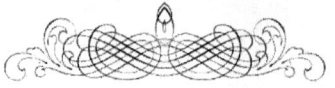

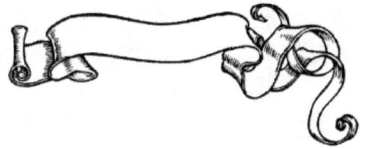

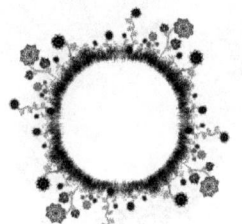

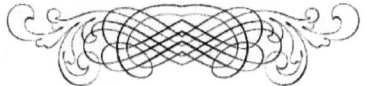

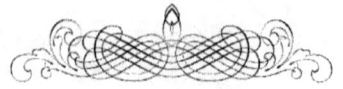

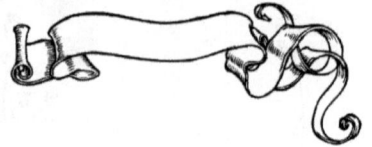

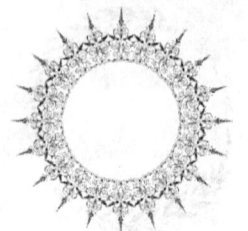

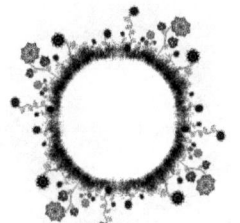

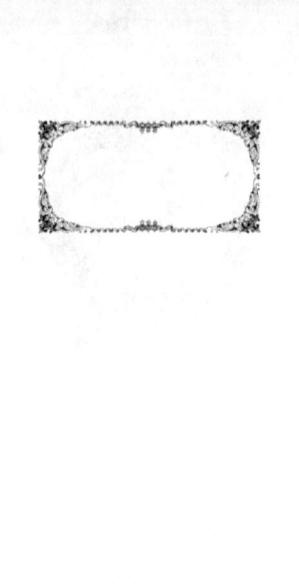

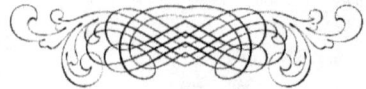

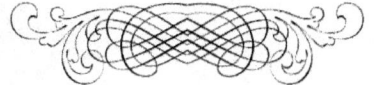

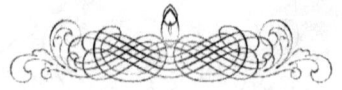

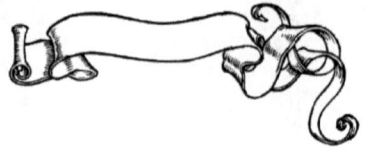

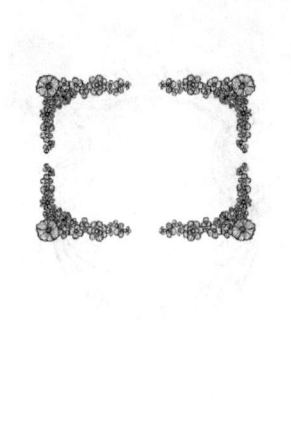

About the Author

Lorelai Hamilton is a seasoned tarot reader with over 13 years of professional experience in the field. Based in the enchanting landscapes of the Pacific Northwest, Lorelai has honed her craft and established herself as a trusted guide in the realm of tarot.

Her passion for tarot led her to create the renowned Living Color Tarot Deck, a vibrant and illuminating tool for spiritual exploration and self-discovery.

Alongside her tarot practice, Lorelai shares her expertise with a global audience. Having conducted readings for individuals across 25 countries, she has cultivated a deep understanding of the universal human experience and the interconnectedness of souls around the world.

Despite her worldly reach, Lorelai remains dedicated to providing personal and insightful readings for clients, offering virtual consultations that resonate with authenticity and compassion. In her journey as a tarot reader, she has been accompanied by her familiar, Ham, whose quiet presence adds an element of magic to her practice.

With a profound commitment to her craft and a heart open to the mysteries of the universe, Lorelai Hamilton continues to illuminate the paths of those who seek guidance, insight, and spiritual clarity through the ancient art of tarot.

www.ingramcontent.com/pod-product-compliance
Lightning Source LLC
Chambersburg PA
CBHW050848160426
43194CB00011B/2067